BLACK LEGACY PRESS™
WWW.BLACKLEGACYPRESS.ORG

SLAVE NARRATIVES

VOLUME XII
OHIO NARRATIVES

By
United States.
Work Projects Administration

Copyright © 2024 by BLACKLEGACYPRESS.ORG

All rights reserved. No part of this publication may be reproduced or transmitted in any form or by any means electronic or mechanical, including information storage and retrieval systems without permission in writing from the publisher, except for student research using the appropriate citations.

ISBN: 978-1-63652-226-5

SLAVE NARRATIVES

A Folk History of Slavery in the United States.
From Interviews with Former Slaves

**UNITED STATES.
WORK PROJECTS ADMINISTRATION**

TYPEWRITTEN RECORDS PREPARED BY
THE FEDERAL WRITERS' PROJECT
1936-1938
ASSEMBLED BY
THE LIBRARY OF CONGRESS PROJECT
WORK PROJECTS ADMINISTRATION
FOR THE DISTRICT OF COLUMBIA
SPONSORED BY THE LIBRARY OF
CONGRESS

WASHINGTON 1941

VOLUME XII
OHIO NARRATIVES

Prepared by
The Federal Writers' Project of
The Works Progress Administration
For the State of Ohio

CONTENTS

CHARLES H. ANDERSON 1
MELISSA BARDEN 9
SUSAN BLEDSOE 11
PHOEBE BOST 15
BEN BROWN 17
SARAH WOODS BURKE 23
JAMES CAMPBELL 27
FLEMING CLARK 33
HANNAH DAVIDSON 39
MARY BELLE DEMPSEY 49
NANCY EAST 51
WADE GLENN 55
DAVID A. HALL 59
CELIA HENDERSON 63
GEORGE JACKSON 71
PERRY SID JEMISON 79
JULIA KING 87
ANGELINE LESTER 93
KISEY MCKIMM 97
THOMAS MCMILLAN 101
SARAH MANN 105
JOHN WILLIAMS MATHEUS 107
JOHN WILLIAMS MATHEUS 113

WILLIAM NELSON	119
CATHERINE SLIM	123
JENNIE SMALL	127
ANNA SMITH	129
NAN STEWART	135
SAMUEL SUTTON	141
RICHARD TOLER	149
JULIA WILLIAMS	157
JULIA WILLIAMS	165
REVEREND WILLIAMS	169
WILLIAM WILLIAMS	175

Ruth Thompson, Interviewing
Graff, Editing

Ex-Slave Interview
Cincinnati

CHARLES H. ANDERSON
3122 Fredonia St.,
Cincinnati, Ohio

CHARLES H. ANDERSON

"Life experience excels all reading. Every place you go, you learn something from every class of people. Books are just for a memory, to keep history and the like, but I don't have to go huntin' in libraries, I got one in my own head, for you can't forget what you learn from experience."

The old man speaking is a living example of his theory, and, judging from his bearing, his experience has given him a philosophical outlook which comprehends love, gentleness and wisdom. Charles H. Anderson, 3122 Fredonia Street, was born December 23, 1845, in Richmond, Virginia, as a slave belonging to J.L. Woodson, grocer, "an exceedingly good owner—not cruel to anyone".

With his mother, father, and 15 brothers and sisters, he lived at the Woodson home in the city, some of the time in a cabin in the rear, but mostly in the "big house". Favored of all the slaves, he was trusted to go to the cash drawer for spending money, and permitted to help himself to candy and all he wanted to eat. With the help of the mistress, his mother made all his clothes, and he was "about as well dressed as anybody".

"I always associated with high-class folks, but I never went to church then, or to school a day in my life. My owner never sent me or my brothers, and then when free schools came in, education wasn't on my mind. I just didn't think about education. Now, I read a few words, and I can write my name. But experience is what counts most."

Tapping the porch floor with his cane for emphasis, the old fellow's softly slurred words fell rapidly but clearly. Sometimes his tongue got twisted, and he had to repeat. Often he had to switch his pipe from one side of his mouth to the other; for, as he explained, "there ain't many tooth-es left in there". Mr. Anderson is rather slight of build, and his features are fine, his bald head shiny, and his eyes bright and eager. Though he says he "ain't much good anymore", he seems half a century old instead of "92 next December, if I can make it".

"I have been having some sick spells lately, snapped three or four ribs out of place several years ago, and was in bed for six weeks after my wife died ten year ago. But my step-daughter here nursed me through it. Doctor says he doesn't see how I keep on living. But they take good care of me, my sons and step-daughter. They live here with me, and we're comfortable."

And comfortable, neat, and clean they are in the trimmest little frame house on the street, painted grey with green trim, having a square of green lawn in front and another in back enclosed with a rail fence, gay flowers in the corners, rubber plants in pots on the porch, and grape arbor down one side of the back yard. Inside, rust-colored mohair overstuffed chairs and davenport look prim with white, crocheted doilies, a big clock with weights stands in one corner on an ornately carved table, and several enlarged framed photographs hang on the wall. The other two rooms are the combined kitchen and dining room, and a bedroom with a heatrola in it "to warm an old man's bones". Additional bedrooms are upstairs.

Pointing to one of the pictures, he remarked, "That was me at 37. Had it taken for my boss where I worked. It was a post card, and then I had it enlarged for myself. That was just before I married Helen".

Helen Comer, nee Cruitt, was a widow with four youngsters when he met her 54 years ago. One year later they were married and had two boys, Charles, now 47, employed as an auto repair man, and Samuel, 43, a sorter in the Post Office, both bachelors.

"Yes sir, I sure was healthy-looking them days. Always was strong, never took a dollars worth of medicine in fifty year or more till I had these last sick spells. But we had good living in slave days. In one sense we were better off then than after the war, 'cause we had plenty to eat. Nowadays, everybody has to fen' for himself, and they'd kill a man for a dime.

"Whip the slaves? Oh, my God! Don't mention it, don't mention it! Lots of 'em in Old Dominion got beatings for punishment. They didn't have no jail for slaves, but the owners used a whip and lash on 'em. I've seen 'am on a chain gang, too, up at the penitentiary. But I never got a whipping in my life. Used to help around the grocery, and deliver groceries. Used to go up to Jeff Davis' house every day. He was a fine man. Always was good to me. But then I never quarreled with anybody, always minded my own business. And I never was scared of nothing. Most folks was superstitious, but I never believed in ghosts nor anything I didn't see. Never wore a charm. Never took much stock in that kind of business. The old people used to carry potatoes to keep off rheumatism. Yes, sir. They had to steal an Irish potato, and carry it till it was hard as a rock; then they'd say they never get rheumatism.

"Saturday was our busy day at the store; but after work, I used to go to the drag downs. Some people say 'hoe down' or 'dig down', I guess 'cause they'd dig right into it, and give it all they got. I was a great hand at fiddlin'. Got one in there now that is 107-year old, but I haven't played for years. Since I broke my shoulder bone, I can't handle the bow. But I used to play at all the drag downs. Anything I heard played once, I could play. Used to play two steps, one of 'em called 'Devil's Dream', and three or four good German waltzes, and 'Turkey in the Straw'—but we didn't call it that then. It was the same piece, but I forget what we called it. They don't play the same nowadays. Playin' now is just a time-consumer, that's all; they got it all tore to pieces, no top or bottom to it.

"We used to play games, too. Ring games at play parties—'Ring Around the Rosie', 'Chase the Squirrel', and 'Holly Golly'. Never hear of Holly Golly? Well, they'd pass around the peanuts, and whoever'd get three nuts in one shell had to give that one to the one who had started the game. Then they'd pass 'em around again. Just a peanut-eating contest, sorta.

"Abraham Lincoln? Well, they's people born in this world for every occupation and Lincoln was a natural born man for the job he completed. Just check it back to Pharoah' time: There was Moses born to deliver the children of Israel. And John Brown, he was born for a purpose. But they said he was cruel all the way th'ough, and they hung him in February, 1859. That created a great sensation. And he said, 'Go ahead. Do your work. I done mine'. Then they whipped around till they got the war started. And that was the start of the Civil War.

"I enlisted April 10, 1865, and was sent to San Diego, Texas; but I never was in a battle. And they was only one time when I felt anyways skittish. That was when I was a new recruit on picket duty. And it was pitch dark, and I heard something comin' th'ough the bushes, and I thought, 'Let 'em come, whoever it is'. And I got my bayonet all ready, and waited. I'se gittin' sorta nervous, and purty soon the bushes opened, and what you think come out? A great big ole hog!

"In June '65, I got a cold one night, and contracted this throat trouble I get—never did get rid of it. Still carry it from the war. Got my first pension on that—$6 a month. Ain't many of us left to get pensions now. They's only 11 veterans left in Cincinnati.

"They used to be the Ku Klux Klan organization. That was the pat-rollers, then they called them the Night Riders, and at one time the Regulators. The 'Ole Dragon', his name was Simons, he had control of it, and that continued on for 50 year till after the war when Garfield was president. Then it sprung up again, now the King Bee is in prison.

"Well, after the war I was free. But it didn't make much difference to me; I just had to work for myself instead of somebody else. And I just rambled around. Sort of a floater. But I always worked, and I always eat regular, and had regular rest. Work never hurt nobody. I lived so many places, Cleveland, and ever'place, but I made it here longer than anyplace—53 year. I worked on the railroad, bossin'. Always had men under me. When the Chesapeake and Ohio put th'ough that extension to White Sulphur, we cut tracks th'ough a tunnel 7 mile long. And I handled men in '83 when they put the C & O th'ough here. But since I was 71, I been doin' handy work—just general handy man. Used to do a lot of carving, too, till I broke my shoulder bone. Carved that ol' pipe of mine 25 year ago out of an ol' umbrella handle, and carved this monkey watch charm. But the last three year I ain't done much of anything.

"Go to church sometimes, over here to the Corinthian Baptis' Church of Walnut Hills. But church don't do much good nowadays. They got too much education for church. This new-fangled education is just a bunch of ignoramacy. Everybody's just looking for a string to pull to get something—not to help others. About one-third goes to see what everbody else is wearing, and who's got the nicest clothes. And they sit back, and they say, 'What she think she look like with that thing on her haid?'. The other two-thirds? Why, they just go for nonsense, I guess. Those who go for religion are scarce as chicken teeth. Yes sir, they go more for sight-seein' than soul-savin'.

"They's so much gingerbread work goin' on now. Our most prominent people come from the eastern part of the United States. All wise people come from the East, just as the wise men did when the Star of Bethlehem appeared when Christ was born. And the farther east you go, the more common knowledge a person's got. That ain't no Dream Boat. Nowadays, people are gettin' crazier everyday. We got too much liberty; it's all 'little you, and big me'. Everybody's got a right to his own opinion, and the old fashioned way was good enough for my father, and it's good enough for me.

"If your back trail is clean, you don't need to worry about the future. Your future life is your past conduct. It's a trailer behind you. And I ain't quite dead yet, efn I do smell bad!"

United States. Work Projects Administration

Slave Narratives

Story and Photo by Frank M. Smith

Ex-Slaves
Mahoning County, District #5
Youngstown, Ohio

The Story of MRS. MELISSA (LOWE) BARDEN, Youngstown, Ohio.

MELISSA BARDEN

Mrs. Melissa (Lowe) Barden of 1671 Jacobs Road, was "bred and born" on the plantation of David Lowe, near Summersville, Georgia, Chattooga County, and when asked how old she was said "I's way up yonder somewheres maybe 80 or 90 years."

Melissa assumed her master's name Lowe, and says he was very good to her and that she loved him. Only once did she feel ill towards him and that was when he sold her mother. She and her sister were left alone. Later he gave her sister and several other slaves to his newly married daughter as a wedding present. This sister was sold and re-sold and when the slaves were given their freedom her mother came to claim her children, but Melissa was the only one of the four she could find. Her mother took her to a plantation in Newton County, where they worked until coming north. The mother died here and Melissa married a man named Barden.

Melissa says she was very happy on the plantation where they danced and sang folk songs of the South, such as "Sho' Fly Go 'Way From Me", and others after their days work was done.

When asked if she objected to having her picture taken she said, "all right, but don't you-all poke fun at me because I am just as God made me."

Melissa lives with her daughter, Nany Hardie, in a neat bungalow on the Sharon Line, a Negro district. Melissa's health is good with the exception of cataracts over her eyes which have caused her to be totally blind.

Ohio Guide
Ex-Slave Stories
Aug 15, 1937

SUSAN BLEDSOE
462-12th St. S.E., Canton, Ohio

SUSAN BLEDSOE

"I was born on a plantation in Gilee County, near the town of Elkton, in Tennessee, on August 15, 1845. My father's name was Shedrick Daley and he was owned by Tom Daley and my mother's name was Rhedia Jenkins and her master's name was Silas Jenkins. I was owned by my mother's master but some of my brothers and sisters—I had six brothers and six sisters—were owned by Tom Daley.

I always worked in the fields with the men except when I was called to the house to do work there. 'Masse' Jenkins was good and kind to all us slaves and we had good times in the evening after work. We got in groups in front of the cabins and sang and danced to the music of banjoes until the overseer would come along and make us go to bed. No, I don't remember what the songs were, nothing in particular, I guess, just some we made up and we would sing a line or two over and over again.

We were not allowed to work on Sunday but we could go to church if we wanted to. There wasn't any colored church but we could go to the white folks church if we went with our overseer. His name was Charlie Bull and he was good to all of us.

Yes, they had to whip a slave sometimes, but only the bad ones, and they deserved it. No, there wasn't any jail on the plantation.

We all had to get up at sunup and work till sundown and we always had good food and plenty of it; you see they had to feed us well so we would be strong. I got better food when I was a slave than I have ever had since.

Our beds were home made, they made them out of poplar wood and gave us straw ticks to sleep on. I got two calico dresses a year and these were my Sunday dresses and I was only allowed to wear them on week days after they were almost worn out. Our shoes were made right on the plantation.

When any slaves got sick, Mr. Bull, the overseer, got a regular doctor and when a slave died we kept right on working until it was time for the funeral, then we were called in but had to go right back to work as soon as it was over. Coffins were made by the slaves out of poplar lumber.

We didn't play many games, the only ones I can remember are 'ball' and 'marbles'. No, they would not let us play 'cards'.

One day I was sent out to clean the hen house and to burn the straw. I cleaned the hen house, pushed the straw up on a pile and set fire to it and burned the hen house down and I sure thought I was going to get whipped, but I didn't, for I had a good 'masse'.

We always got along fine with the children of the slave owners but none of the colored people would have anything to do with the 'poor white trash' who were too poor to own slaves and had to do their own work.

There was never any uprisings on our plantations and I never heard about any around where I lived. We were all happy and contented and had good times.

Yes, I can remember when we were set free. Mr. Bull told us and we cut long poles and fastened balls of cotton on the ends and set fire to them. Then, we run around with them burning, a-singin' and a-dancin'. No, we did not try to run away and never left the plantation until Mr. Bull said we could go.

After the war, I worked for Mr. Bull for about a year on the old plantation and was treated like one of the family. After that I worked for my brother on a little farm near the old home place. He was buying his farm from his master, Mr. Tom Daley.

I was married on my brother's place to Wade Bledsoe in 1870. He has been dead now about 15 years. His master had given him a small farm but I do not remember his master's name. Yes, I lived in Tennessee until after my husband died. I came to Canton in 1929 to live with my granddaughter, Mrs. Algie Clark.

I had three children; they are all dead but I have 6 grandchildren, 8 great-grandchildren and 9 great-great-grandchildren, all living. No, I don't think the children today are as good as they used to be, they are just not raised like we were and do too much as they please.

I can't read or write as none of we slaves ever went to school but I used to listen to the white folks talk and copied after them as much as I could."

NOTE: The above is almost exactly as Mrs. Bledsoe talked to our interviewer. Although she is a woman of no schooling she talks well and uses the common negro dialect very little. She is 92 years of age but her mind is clear and she is very entertaining. She receives an Old Age Pension. (Interviewed by Chas. McCullough.)

Story and Photo by Frank Smith

Topic: Ex-slaves
Mahoning County, District #5
Youngstown, Ohio

The Story of MRS. PHOEBE BOST, of Youngstown, Ohio.

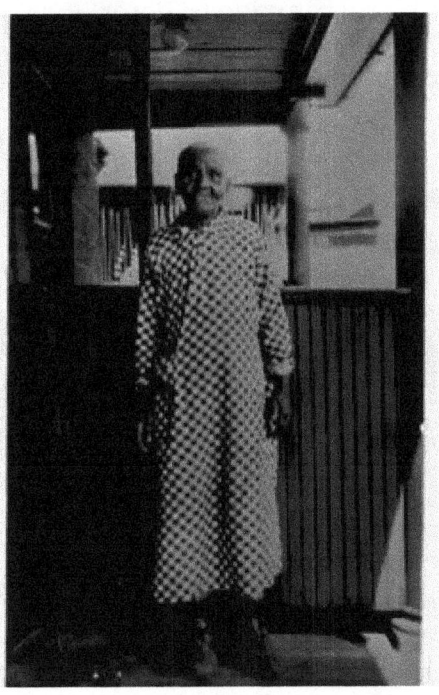

PHOEBE BOST

Mrs. Phoebe Bost, was born on a plantation in Louisiana, near New Orleans. She does not know her exact age but says she was told, when given her freedom that she was about 15 years of age. Phoebe's first master was a man named Simons, who took her to a slave auction in Baltimore, where she was sold to Vaul Mooney (this name is spelled as pronounced, the correct spelling not known.) When Phoebe was given her freedom she assumed the name of Mooney, and went to Stanley County, North Carolina, where she worked for wages until she came north and married to Peter Bost. Phoebe claims both her masters were very mean and would administer a whipping at the slightest provocation.

Phoebe's duties were that of a nurse maid. "I had to hol' the baby all de time she slept" she said "and sometimes I got so sleepy myself I had to prop ma' eyes open with pieces of whisks from a broom."

She claims there was not any recreation, such as singing and dancing permitted at this plantation.

Phoebe, who is now widowed, lives with her daughter, in part of a double house, at 3461 Wilson Avenue, Campbell, Ohio. Their home is fairly well furnished and clean in appearance. Phoebe is of slender stature, and is quite active in spite of the fact that she is nearing her nineties.

WPA in Ohio
By Albert I Dugan [TR: also reported as Dugen]
Jun 9, 1937

Topic: Ex-slaves
Muskingum County, District #2

BEN BROWN
Ex-slave, 100 years
Keen St., Zanesville, Ohio

BEN BROWN

Yes suh I wuz a slave in Vaginyah, Alvamaul (Albermarle) county an' I didn't have any good life, I'm tellin' you dat! It wuz a tough life. I don't know how old I am, dey never told me down dere, but the folks here say I'm a hunderd yeah old an' I spect dats about right. My fathah's name wuz Jack Brown and' my mammy's Nellie Brown. Dey wuz six of us chillun, one sistah Hannah an' three brothers, Jim, Harrison, an' Spot. Jim wuz de oldes an' I wuz next. We wuz born on a very lauge plantation an dey wuz lots an' lots of other slaves, I don't know how many. De log cabins what we live in[HW:?] on both sides de path make it look like a town. Mastah's house wuz a big, big one an' had big brick chimneys on de outside. It wuz a frame house, brown, an' set way back from de road, an' behind dat wuz de slaves' quarters. De mastah, he wuz Fleming Moon an' dey say he wuz cap'n in de wah of 1812. De missy wuz Parley Moon and dey had one son an fouh daughters.

All us chillun an mammy live in a log cabin dat wuz

lauge enuf foh us an we sleep in good beds, tall ones an' low ones dat went undaneath, trundles dey call 'em, and de covahs wuz comfohtable. De mammies did de cookin. We et cohn bread, beans, soup, cabbage an' some othah vegtubles, an a little meat an fish, not much. Cohn cake wuz baked in de ashes, ash-cake we call 'em an' dey wuz good and sweet. Sometimes we got wheat bread, we call dat "seldom bread" an' cohn bread wuz called "common" becos we had it ev'ry day. A boss mammy, she looked aftah de eatins' and believe me nobuddy got too much.

De meat house wuz full of smoked po'k, but we only got a little piece now an' den. At hog killin' time we built a big fiah an put on stones an' when dey git hot we throw 'em in a hogshead dat has watah in it. Den moah hot stones till de watah is jus right for takin' de hair off de hogs, lots of 'em. Salt herrin' fish in barls cum to our place an we put em in watah to soak an den string em on pointed sticks an' hang up to dry so dey wont be so salty. A little wuz given us with de other food.

I worked about de place doin' chores an takin' care of de younger chillun, when mammy wuz out in de fields at harvest time, an' I worked in de fields too sometimes. De mastah sent me sometimes with young recruits goin' to de army headquartahs at Charlottesville to take care of de horses an show de way. We all worked hard an' when supper wuz ovah I wuz too tired to do anything but go to bed. It wuz jus work, eat an sleep foh most of us, dere wuz no time foh play. Some of em tried to sing or tell stories or pray but dey soon went to bed. Sometimes I heard some of de stories about hants and speerits an devils that skeered me so I ran to bed an' covered mah head.

Mastah died an' den missie, she and a son-in-law took charge of de place. Mah sistah Hannah wuz sold on de auction block at Richmon to Mastah Frank Maxie (Massie?) an' taken to de plantation near Charlottesville. I missed mah sistah terrible an ran away to see her, ran away three times, but ev'ry time dey cum on horseback an git me jus befoh I got to Maxies. The missie wuz with dem on a horse and she ax where I goin an' I told her. Mah hands wuz tied crossways in front with a big rope so hard it hurt. Den I wuz left on de groun foh a long time while missie visited Missie Maxie. Dey start home on horses pulling de rope tied to mah hands. I had to run or fall down an' be dragged on de groun'. It wuz terrible. When we got home de missie whipped me with a thick hickory switch an' she wasn't a bit lenient. I wuz whipped ev'ry time I ran away to see mah sister.

When dere wuz talk of Yankies cumin' de missie told me to git a box an she filled it with gold an' silver, lots of it, she wuz rich, an I dug a hole near de hen house an put in de box an' covered it with dirt an' smoothed it down an scattered some leaves an twigs ovah it. She told me nevah, nevah to tell about it and I nevah did until now. She showed me a big white card with writin' on it an' said it say "This is a Union Plantation" an' put it on a tree so the Yankies wouldn't try to find de gold and silvers. But I never saw any Yankie squads cum around. When de wah wuz ovah, de missie nevah tell me dat I wuz free an' I kep' on workin' same as befoh. I couldn't read or write an' to me all money coins wuz a cent, big copper cents, dey wuz all alike to me. De slaves wuz not allowed any learnin an' if any books, papers or pictures wuz foun' among us we wuz whipped if we couldn't explain where dey cum from. Mah sistah an' brother cum foh me an tell me I am free and take me with them to Mastah Maxies' place where dey workin. Dey had a big dinnah ready foh me, but I wuz too excited to eat. I worked foh Mastah Maxie too, helpin' with de horses an' doin' chores. Mammy cum' an wuz de cook. I got some clothes and a few cents an' travelers give me small coins foh tending dere horses an' I done done odd jobs here an dere.

I wanted some learnin but dere wuz no way to git it until a white man cleared a place in de woods an' put up branches to make shade. He read books to us foh a while an' den gave it up. A lovly white woman, Missy Holstottle, her husband's name wuz Dave, read a book to me an' I remember de stories to dis day. It wuz called "White an' Black." Some of de stories made me cry.

After wanderin about doin work where I could git it I got a job on de C an O Railroad workin' on de tracks. In Middleport, dat's near Pomeroy, Ohio, I wuz married to Gertie Nutter, a widow with two chillun, an dere wuz no moah chilluns. After mah wife died I wandered about workin' on railroads an' in coal mines an' I wuz hurt in a mine near Zanesville. Felt like mah spine wuz pulled out an I couldn't work any moah an' I cum to mah neice's home here in Zanesville. I got some compensation at first, but not now. I get some old age pension, a little, not much, but I'm thankful foh dat.

Mah life wuz hard an' sad, but now I'm comfortable here with kind friens. I can't read or write, but I surely enjoy de radio. Some nights I dream about de old slave times an' I hear dem cryin' an' prayin', "Oh, Mastah, pray Oh, mastah, mercy!" when dey are bein' whipped, an' I wake up cryin.' I set here in dis room and can remember mos' all of de old life, can see it as plain as day, de hard work, de plantation, de whippings, an' de misery. I'm sure glad it's all over.

United States. Work Projects Administration

James Immel, Reporter

Folklore
Washington County, District Three

SARAH WOODS BURKE
Aged 85

SARAH WOODS BURKE

"Yessir, I guess you all would call me an ex-slave cause I was born in Grayson County, West Virginia and on a plantation I lived for quite a spell, that is until when I was seven years old when we all moved up here to Washington county."

"My Pappy's old Mammy was supposed to have been sold into slavery when my Pappy was one month old and some poor white people took him ter raise. We worked for them until he was a growed up man, also 'til they give him his free papers and 'lowed him to leave the plantation and come up here to the North."

"How did we live on the plantation? Well—you see it was like this we lived in a log cabin with the ground for floors and the beds were built against the walls jus' like bunks. I 'member that the slaves had a hard time getting food, most times they got just what was left over or whatever the slaveholder wanted to give them so at night they would slip outa their cabins on to the plantation and kill a pig, a sheep or some cattle which they would butcher in the woods and cut up. The wimmin folks would carry the pieces back to the cabins in their aprons while the men would stay behind and bury the head, skin and feet."

"Whenever they killed a pig they would have to skin it, because they didn't dare to build a fire. The women folk after getting home would put the meat in special dug trenches and the men would come erlong and cover it up."

"The slave holders in the port of the country I came from was men and it was quite offen that slaves were tied to a whipping stake and whipped with a blacksnake until the blood ran down their bodies."

"I remembers quite clearly one scene that happened jus' afore I left that there part of the country. At the slaveholders home on the plantation I was at it was customary for the white folks to go to church on Sunday morning and to leave the cook in charge. This cook had a habit of making cookies and handing them out to the slaves before the folks returned. Now it happened that on one Sunday for some reason or tother the white folks returned before the regular time and the poor cook did not have time to get the cookies to the slaves so she just hid then in a drawer that was in a sewing chair."

"The white folks had a parrot that always sat on top of a door in this room and when the mistress came in the room the mean old bird hollered out at the top of his voice, 'Its in the rocker. It's in the rocker'. Well the Missus found the cookies and told her husband where upon the husband called his man that done the whipping and they tied the poor cook to the stake and whipped her till she fainted. Next morning the parrot was found dead and a slave was accused because he liked the woman that had been whipped the day before. They whipped him than until the blood ran down his legs."

"Spirits? Yessir I believe in them, but we warnt bothered so much by them in them days but we was by the wild animals. Why after it got dark we children would have to stay indoors for fear of them. The men folks would build a big fire and I can remember my Pappy a settin on top of the house at night with a old flint lock across his legs awaiting for one of them critters to come close enough so he could shoot it. The reason for him being trusted with a gun was because he had been raised by the poor white man who worked for the slaveholder. My Pappy did not work in the fields but drove a team of horses."

"I remembers that when we left the plantation and come to Washington County, Ohio that we traveled in a covered wagon that had big white horse hitched to it. The man that owned the horse was Blake Randolls. He crossed the river 12 miles below Parkersberg. W. Va. on a ferry and went to Stafford, Ohio, in Monroe County where we lived until I was married at the age of 15 to Mr. Burke, by the Justice of the Peace, Edward Oakley. A year later we moved to Curtis Ridge which is seven miles from Stafford and we lived their for say 20 year or more. We moved to Rainbow for a spell and then in 1918 my husband died. The old man hard luck came around cause three years my home burned to the ground and then I came here to live with my boy Joe and his family."

"Mr. Burke and myself raised a family of 16 chilluns and at that time my husband worked at farming for other people at $2.00 a month and a few things they would give him."

"My Pappy got his education from the boy of the white man he lived with because he wasn't allowed to go to school and the white boy was very smart and taught him just as he learned. My Pappy, fought in the Civil War too. On which side? Well, sho nuff on the site of the North, boy."

Hallie Miller, Reporter
Audrey Meighen, Author-Editor

Folklore: Ex-slaves
Gellia County, District 3

JAMES CAMPBELL
Age 86

JAMES CAMPBELL

"Well, I'se bo'n Monro' County, West Virginia, on January 15, 1852, jes' few miles from Union, West Virginia."

"My mammy wuz Dinnah Alexander Campbell an' my pappy wuz Levi Campbell an' dey bof cum frum Monro' County. Dat's 'bout only place I heerd dem speak 'bout."

"Der wuz Levi, Floyd, Henry, Noah, an' Nancy, jes' my haf brudders an' sistahs, but I neber knowed no diffrunce but whut dey wuz my sistahs an' brudders."

"Where we liv? On Marsa John Alexander's farm, he wuz a good Marsa too. All Marsa John want wuz plenty wurk dun and we dun it too, so der wuz no trubble on ouah plantashun. I neber reclec' anyone gittin' whipped or bad treatment frum him. I does 'members, dat sum de neighbers say dey wuz treated prutty mean, but I don't 'member much 'bout it 'caise I'se leetle den."

"Wher'd I sleep? I neber fergit dat trun'l bed, dat I sleep in.

"Marsa John's place kinda stock farm an' I dun de milkin'. You all know dat wuz easy like so I jes' keep busy milkin' an' gits out de hard work. Nudder thing I lik to do wuz pick berries, dat wuz easy too, so I dun my shar' pickin'."

"Money? Lawsy chile, I neber dun seen eny money 'til aftah I dun cum to Gallipolis aftah der war. An' how I lik' to heah it jingle, if I jes' had two cents, I'd make it jingle."

"We all had plenty an' good things to eat, beans, corn, tatahs, melons an' hot mush, corn bread; we jes' seen white flour wunce in a while."

"Yes mam, we had rabbit, wil' turkey, pheasunts, an' fish, say I'se tellin' you-all dat riful pappy had shure cud kill de game."

"Nudder good ole time wuz maple sugar makin' time, mostly dun at night by limestone burnin'. Yes, I heped with the 'lasses an' all de time I wuz a thinkin' 'bout dem hot biscets, ham meat, corn bread an' 'lasses."

"We liv in a cabin on Marse John's place. Der wuzn't much in de cabin but my mammy kept it mighty clean. Say, I kin see dat ole' fiah place wid de big logs a burnin' right now; uh, an' smell dat good cookin', all dun in iron pots an' skillets. An' all de cookin' an' heatin' wuz dun by wood, why I nebber seed a lump o' coal all time I wuz der. We all had to cut so much wood an' pile it up two weeks 'for Christmas, an' den when ouah pile wuz cut, den ouah wurk wuz dun, so we'd jes' hav good time."

"We all woah jeans clos', jes pants an' jacket. In de summah we chilluns all went barefoot, but in de wintah we all woah shoes."

"Ol' Marse John an' his family liv in a big fine brick hous'. Marse John had des chilluns, Miss Betty an' Miss Ann an' der wuz Marse Mike an' Marse John. Marse John, he wuz sorta spiled lik. He dun wen to de war an' runs 'way frum Harpers Ferry an' cum home jes' sceered to death. He get himsef a pah o' crutches an' neber goes back. Marse John dun used dem crutches 'til aftah de war wuz ovah. Den der wuz ol' Missy Kimberton—de gran'muthah. She wuz 'culiar but prutty good, so wuz Marse's chilluns."

"Ol' Marse John had bout 20 slaves so de wurk wuzn't so bad on nun ob us. I kin jes' see dem ol' bindahs and harrows now, dat dey used den. It would shure look funny usin' 'em now."

"I all'us got up foah clock in de mornin' to git in de cows an' I didn't hurry nun, 'caise dat tak in de time."

"Ouah mammy neber 'lowed de old folks to tell us chilluns sceery stories o' hants an' sich lik' so der's nun foah me to 'member."

"Travelin' wuz rather slo' lik. De only way wuz in ox-carts or on hoss back. We all didn't hav much time fer travelin'. Our Marse wuz too good to think 'bout runnin' 'way."

"Nun my fam'ly cud read er write. I lurned to read an write aftah I cum up Norf to Ohio. Dat wuz biggest thing I ebber tackled, but it made me de happies' aftah I learn't."

"We all went to Sunday School an' meetin'. Yes mam, we had to wurk on Sundays, too, if we did hav any spare time, we went visit in'. On Saturday nights we had big time foah der wuz mos' all'us dancin' an' we'd dance long as de can'les lasted. Can'les wuz all we had any time fur light."

"I 'member one de neighbah boys tried to run 'way an' de patrollahs got 'im an' fetched 'im back an' he shure dun got a wallopin' fer it. Dat dun tuk any sich notion out my head. Dem patrollahs dun keep us skeered to deaf all de time. One, Henry Jones, runned off and went cleah up Norf sum place an' dey neber did git 'im. 'Course we all wuz shure powahful glad 'bout his 'scapin'."

"We'se neber 'lowed out de cabin at night. But sum times de oldah 'uns wud sneak out at night an'tak de hosses an' tak a leetle ride. An' man it wud bin jes' too bad if ol' Marse John ketched 'em: dat wuz shure heaps o' fun fer de kids. I 'member hearin' wunce de ol' folks talkin' 'bout de way one Marse dun sum black boys dat dun sumthin' wrong. He jes' mak 'em bite off de heads o' baccer wurms; mysef I'd ruther tuk a lickin."

"On Christmus Day, we'd git fiah crackahs an' drink brandy, dat wuz all. Dat day wuz only one we didn't wurk. On Saturday evenin's we'd mold candles, dat wuzn't so bad."

"De happies' time o' my life wuz when Cap'n Tipton, a Yankee soljer cumed an' tol' us de wah wuz ober an' we wuz free. Cap'n. Tipton sez, "Youse de boys we dun dis foah". We shure didn't lose no time gittin' 'way; no man."

"We went to Lewisburg an' den up to Cha'leston by wagon an' den tuk de guvment boat, Genrul Crooks, an' it brung us heah to Gallipolis in 1865. Dat Ohio shoah shure looked prutty."

"I'se shure thankful to Mr. Lincoln foah whut he dun foah us folks, but dat Jeff Davis, well I ain't sayin' whut I'se thinkin'."

"De is jes' like de worl', der is lots o' good an' lots o' bad in it."

United States. Work Projects Administration

WPA in Ohio
Federal Writers' Project

Topic: Ex-Slavery
Jefferson Co, District #2

FLEMING CLARK
Ex-Slave, 74+ in years

FLEMING CLARK

My father's name wuz Fleming Clark and my mother's name wuz Emmaline Clark. Both of dem wuz in slavery. Der massa's name wuz David Bowers. I don't know where dey cum from but dey moved to Bad Creek after slavery days.

Der wuz three of us chillun. Charles, de oldest, den Anthony next and den me, de youngest. I wuz workin' for a white man and wuz old enough to drive cows and work in de 'bacco fields, pickin' worms off de leaves. De other brudders worked wid my father on another plantation. De house where I lived wid de white Massa Lewis Northsinge and his Missus, wuz a log house wid just two rooms. I had just a little straw tick and a cot dat de massa made himself and I hed a common quilt dat de missus made to cover me.

I hear dat my grandmother died during slavery and dat my grandfather wuz killed by his massa during slavery.

On Sunday I would go home and stay wid my father and mother and two brothers. We would play around wid ball and marbles. We had no school or church. We were too far away for church.

I earned no money. All I got wus just my food and clothes. I wuz leasted out to my massa and missus. I ate corn bread, fat hog meat and drank butter milk. Sometimes my father would catch possum and my mother would cook them, and bring me over a piece. I used to eat rabbit and fish. Dey used to go fishin' in de creek. I liked rabbit and groundhog. De food wuz boiled and roasted in de oven. De slaves have a little patch for a garden and day work it mostly at night when it wuz moonlight.

We wore geans and shirts of yellow cotton, we wore no shoes up til Christmas. I wore just de same during de summer except a little coat. We had no under shirt lik we have now. We wore de same on Sunday. Der wuz no Sunday suit.

De mass and missus hed one boy. De boy wuz much older than I. Dey were all kind to me. I remember plenty poor white chillun. I remember Will and John Nathan. Dey were poor white people.

My massa had three plantations. He had five slaves on one and four on another. I worked on one with four slaves. My father worked on one wid my brother and mother. We would wake up at 4 and 5 o'clock and do chores in de barn by lamp light. De overseer would ring a bell in de yeard, if it wuz not too cold to go out. If it wuz too cold he would cum and knock on de door. It wuz 8 or 9 o'clock fore we cum in at night. Den we have to milk de cows to fore we have supper.

De slaves were punished fore cumin' in too soon and

unhitching de horses. Dey would bend dem accross a barrel and switch dem and den send dem back to de fields.

I head dem say dey switch de blood out of dem and salt de wound den dey could not work de next day.

I saw slaves sold. Dey would stand on a block and men would bid for dem. De highest bidder bought de slaves. I saw dem travel in groups, not chained, one white man in front and one in back. Dey looked like cattle.

De white folks never learned me to read or write.

Der were petrollers. Dey were mean if dey catch you out late at night. If a slave wus out late at night he had to have a notice from his massa. Der wuz trouble if de slaves were out late at night or if dey run off to another man.

De slaves worked on Saturday afternoons. Dey stay in de cabins on Saturday nights and Sundays. We worked on New Years day. De massa would give us a little hard cider on Christmas day. Dey would give a big supper at corn huskin' or cotton pickin' and give a little play or somethin' lik dat.

I remember two weddings. Dey hed chicken, and mutton to eat and corn bread. Dey all ganged round de table. Der wur milk and butter. I remember one wedding of de white people. I made de ice cream for dem. I remember playin' marbles and ball.

Sometimes a racer snake would run after us, wrap round us and whip us with its tail. The first one I remember got after me in de orchard. He wrapped right round me and whipped me with his tail.

My mother took care of de slaves when dey were

sick. You had to be awful sick if dey didn't make you go out. Dey made der own medicine in those days. We used asafetida and put a piece in a bag and hung it round our necks. It wuz supposed to keep us from ketchin' diseases from anyone else.

When freedom cum dey were all shoutin' and I run to my mother and asked her what it wuz all bout. De white man said you are all free and can go. I remember the Yankee soldier comin' through the wheat field.

My parents lived very light de first year after de war. We lived in a log cabin. De white man helped dem a little. My father went to work makin' charcoal. Der wuz no school for Negroes and no land that I remember.

I married Alice Thompson. She wuz 16 and I wuz 26. We hed a little weddin' down in Bushannon, Virginny. A Baptist preacher named Shirley married us. Der were bout a dozen at de weddin'. We hed a little dancin' and banjo play in'. I hed two chillun but dey died and my wife died a long, long time ago.

I just heard a little bout Abraham Lincoln. I believe he wuz a good man. I just hed a slight remembrance of Abraham Lincoln and Jefferson Davis. I have heard of Booker T. Washington, felt just de same bout him. A pretty good man.

I think it wuz a great thing that slavery anded, I would not lik to see it now.

I joined de Baptist church but I have been runnin' round from place to place. We always prosper and get along with our fellowmen if we are religious.

De overseer wuz poor white trash. His rules were you hed to be out on de plantation before daylight. Sometimes we hed to sit around on de fence to wait for daylight and we did not go in before dark. We go in bout one for meals.

United States. Work Projects Administration

K. Osthimer, Author
Aug 12, 1937

Folklore: Stories from Ex-Slaves
Lucas County, District Nine
Toledo, Ohio

The Story of MRS. HANNAH DAVIDSON.

HANNAH DAVIDSON

Mrs. Hannah Davidson occupies two rooms in a home at 533 Woodland Avenue, Toledo, Ohio. Born on a plantation in Ballard County, Kentucky, in 1852, she is today a little, white-haired old lady. Dark, flashing eyes peer through her spectacles. Always quick to learn, she has taught herself to read. She says, "I could always spell almost everything." She has eagerly sought education. Much of her ability to read has been gained from attendance in recent years in WPA "opportunity classes" in the city. Today, this warm-hearted, quiet little Negro woman ekes out a bare existence on an old age pension of $23.00 a month. It is with regret that she recalls the shadows and sufferings of the past. She says, "It is best not to talk about them. The things that my sister May and I suffered were so terrible that people would not believe them. It is best not to have such things in our memory."

"My father and mother were Isaac and Nancy Meriwether," she stated. "All the slaves went under the name of my master and mistress, Emmett and Susan Meriwether. I had four sisters and two brothers. There was Adeline, Dorah, Alice, and Lizzie. My brothers were Major and George Meriwether. We lived in a log cabin made of sticks and dirt, you know, logs and dirt stuck in the cracks. We slept on beds made of boards nailed up.

"I don't remember anything about my grandparents. My folks were sold around and I couldn't keep track of them.

"The first work I did out from home was with my mistress's brother, Dr. Jim Taylor, in Kentucky, taking care of his children. I was an awful tiny little somethin' about eight or nine years old. I used to turn the reel for the old folks who was spinning. That's all I've ever known—work.

"I never got a penny. My master kept me and my sister Mary twenty-two long years after we were supposed to be free. Work, work, work. I don't think my sister and I ever went to bed before twelve o'clock at night. We never got a penny. They could have spared it, too; they had enough.

"We ate corn bread and fat meat. Meat and bread, we kids called it. We all had a pint tin cup of buttermilk. No slaves had their own gardens.

"The men just wore jeans. The slaves all made their own clothes. They just wove all the time; the old women wove all the time. I wasn't old enough to go in the field like the oldest children. The oldest children—they worked. After slavery ended, my sister Mary and me worked as ex-slaves, and we worked. Most of the slaves had shoes, but us kids used to run around barefoot most of the time.

"My folks, my master and mistress, lived in a great, white, frame house, just the same as a hotel. I grew up with the youngest child, Mayo. The other white children grew up and worked as overseers. Mayo always wanted me to call him 'Master Mayo'. I fought him all the time. I never would call him 'Master Mayo'. My mistress wouldn't let anyone harm me and she made Mayo behave.

"My master wouldn't let the poor white neighbors—no one—tell us we was free. The plantation was many, many acres, hundreds and hundreds of acres, honey. There were about twenty-five or thirty families of slaves. They got up and stood until daylight, waiting to plow. Yes, child, they was up early. Our folks don't know how we had to work. I don't like to tell you how we were treated—how we had to work. It's best to brush those things out of our memory.

"If you wanted to go to another plantation, you had to have a pass. If my folks was going to somebody's house, they'd have to have a pass. Otherwise they'd be whipped. They'd take a big man and tie his hands behind a tree, just like that big tree outside, and whip him with a rawhide and draw blood every whip. I know I was scared every time I'd hear the slave say, 'Pray, Master.'

"Once, when I was milking a cow, I asked Master Ousley, 'Master Ousley, will you do me a favor?'

"He said in his drawl, 'Of course I will.'

"'Take me to McCracken County,' I said. I didn't even know where McCracken County was, but my sister was there. I wanted to find my sister. When I reached the house where my sister stayed, I went through the gate. I asked if this was the house where Mary Meriwether lived. Her mistress said, 'Yes, she's in the back. Are you the girl Mr. Meriwether's looking for?" My heart was in my mouth. It just seemed I couldn't go through the gate. I never even saw my sister that time. I hid for a while and then went back.

"We didn't have any churches. My master would come down Sunday morning with just enough flour to make bread. Coffee, too. Their coffee was parts of meal, corn and so on. Work all week and that's what they had for coffee.

"We used to sing, 'Swing low, sweet chariot'. When our folks sang that, we could really see the chariot.

"Once, Jim Ferguson, a colored man, came to teach school. The white folks beat and whipped him and drove him away in his underwear.

"I wanted so hard to learn to read, but I didn't even know I was free, even when slavery was ended.

"I been so exhausted working, I was like an inch-worm crawling along a roof. I worked till I thought another lick would kill me. If you had something to do, you did it or got whipped. Once I was so tired I couldn't work any more. I crawled in a hole under the house and stayed there till I was rested. I didn't get whipped, either.

"I never will forget it—how my master always used to say, 'Keep a nigger down' I never will forget it. I used to wait on table and I heard them talk.

"The only fun we had was on Sunday evening, after work. That was the only chance we got. We used to go away off from the house and play in the haystack.

"Our folks was so cruel, the slaves used to whisper

'round. Some of them knew they was free, even if the white folks didn't want 'em to find out they was free. They went off in the woods sometimes. But I was just a little kid and I wasn't allowed to go around the big folks.

"I seen enough what the old folks went through. My sister and I went through enough after slavery was over. For twenty-one long years we were enslaved, even after we were supposed to be free. We didn't even know we were free. We had to wash the white people's feet when they took their shoes off at night—the men and women.

"Sundays the slaves would wash out their clothes. It was the only time they had to themselves. Some of the old men worked in their tobacco patches. We never observed Christmas. We never had no holidays, son, no, sir! We didn't know what the word was.

"I never saw any slave funerals. Some slaves died, but I never saw any of them buried. I didn't see any funerals at all.

"The white folks would come down to the cabins to marry the slaves. The master or mistress would read a little out of a book. That's all there was to it.

"We used to play a game called 'Hulgul'. We'd play it in the cabins and sometimes with the white children. We'd hold hazelnuts in our hands. I'd say 'Hulgul' How many? You'd guess. If you hit it right, you'd get them all and it would be your turn to say 'Hulgul'. If you'd say 'Three!' and I only had two, you'd have to give me another to make three.

"The kids nowadays can go right to the store and buy a ball to play with. We'd have to make a ball out of yarn and put a sock around it for a cover. Six of us would stay on one side of a house and six on the other side. Then we'd throw the ball over the roof and say 'Catch!' If you'd catch it you'd run around to the; other side and hit somebody, then start over. We worked so hard we couldn't play long on Sunday evenings.

"School? We never seen the inside of a schoolhouse. Mistress used to read the Bible to us every Sunday morning.

"We say two songs I still remember.

> "I think when I read that sweet story of old,
> When Jesus was here among men,
> How he called little children like lambs to his fold,
> I should like to have been with them then.
>
> "I wish that his hands had been placed on my head,
> That his arms had been thrown around me,
> That I might have seen his kind face when he said
> 'Let the little ones come unto me.'
>
> "Yet still to his footstool in prayer I nay go
> And ask for a share of his love,
> And that I might earnestly seek Him below
> And see Him and hear Him above.

"Then there was another:

> "I want to be an angel
> And with the angels stand
> With a crown upon my Forehead
> And a harp within my hand.

"And there before my Saviour,
So glorious and so bright,
I'd make the sweetest music
And praise him day and night.

"And as soon as we got through singing those songs, we had to get right out to work. I was always glad when they called us in the house to Sunday school. It was the only chance we'd get to rest.

"When the slaves got sick, they'd take and look after themselves. My master had a whole wall of his house for medicine, just like a store. They made their own medicines and pills. My mistress's brother, Dr. Jim Taylor, was a doctor. They done their own doctoring. I still have the mark where I was vaccinated by my master.

"People was lousy in them days. I always had to pick louses from the heads of the white children. You don't find children like that nowadays.

"My mistress had a little roan horse. She went all through the war on that horse. Us little kids never went around the big folks. We didn't watch folks faces to learn, like children do now. They wouldn't let us. All I know about the Civil War was that it was goin' on. I heard talk about killin' and so on, but I didn't know no thin' about it.

"My mother was the last slave to get off the plantation. She travelled across the plantation all night with us children. It was pouring rain. The white folks surrounded her and took away us children, and gave her so many minutes to get off the plantation. We never saw her again. She died away from us.

"My brother came to see us once when slavery was over. He was grown up. My master wasn't going to let him see us and he took up his gun. My mistress said he should let him see us. My brother gave me a little coral ring. I thought it was the prettiest thing I ever saw.

"I made my sister leave. I took a rolling pin to make her go and she finally left. They didn't have any more business with us than you have right now.

"I remember when Yankee soldiers came riding through the yard. I was scared and ran away crying. I can see them now. Their swords hung at their sides and their horses walked proud, as if they walked on their hind legs. The master was in the field trying to hide his money and guns and things. The soldiers said, 'We won't hurt you, child.' It made me feel wonderful.

"What I call the Ku Klux were those people who met at night and if they heard anybody saying you was free, they would take you out at night and whip you. They were the plantation owners. I never saw them ride, but I heard about them and what they did. My master used to tell us he wished he knew who the Ku Kluxers were. But he knew, all right, I used to wait on table and I heard them talking. 'Gonna lynch another nigger tonight!'

"The slaves tried to get schools, but they didn't get any. Finally they started a few schools in little log cabins. But we children, my sister and I, never went to school.

"I married William L. Davison, when I was thirty-two years old. That was after I left the plantation. I never had company there. I had to work. I have only one grandchild still living, Willa May Reynolds. She taught school in City Grove, Tennessee. She's married now.

"I thought Abe Lincoln was a great man. What little I know about him, I always thought he was a great man. He did a lot of good.

"Us kids always used to sing a song, 'Gonna hang Jeff Davis to a sour apple tree as we go marchin' home.' I didn't know what it meant at the time.

"I never knew much about Booker T. Washington, but I heard about him. Frederick Douglass was a great man, too. He did lots of good, like Abe Lincoln.

"Well, slavery's over and I think that's a grand thing. A white lady recently asked me, 'Don't you think you were better off under the white people?' I said 'What you talkin' about? The birds of the air have their freedom'. I don't know why she should ask me that anyway.

"I belong to the Third Baptist Church. I think all people should be religious. Christ was a missionary. He went about doing good to people. You should be clean, honest, and do everything good for people. I first turn the searchlight on myself. To be a true Christian, you must do as Christ said: 'Love one another'. You know, that's why I said I didn't want to tell about my life and the terrible things that I and my sister Mary suffered. I want to forgive those people. Some people tell me those people are in hell now. But I don't think that. I believe we should all do good to everybody."

United States. Work Projects Administration

Betty Lugabell, Reporter [TR: also reported as Lugabill]
Harold Pugh, Editor
R.S. Drum, Supervisor
Jun 9, 1937

Folklore: Ex-Slaves
Paulding Co., District 10

MARY BELLE DEMPSEY
Ex-Slave, 87 years

MARY BELLE DEMPSEY

"I was only two years old when my family moved here, from Wilford county, Kentucky. 'Course I don't remember anything of our slave days, but my mother told me all about it."

"My mother and father were named Sidney Jane and William Booker. I had one brother named George William Booker."

"The man who owned my father and mother was a good man." He was good to them and never 'bused them. He had quite a large plantation and owned 26 slaves. Each slave family had a house of their own and the women of each family prepared the meals, in their cabins. These cabins were warm and in good shape."

"The master farmed his land and the men folks helped in the fields but the women took care of their homes."

"We had our churches, too. Sometimes the white folks would try to cause trouble when the negroes were holding their meetings, then a night the men of the church would place chunks and matches on the white folks gate post. In the morning the white folks would find them and know that it was a warning if they din't quit causing trouble their buildings would be burned."

"There was a farm that joined my parents' master's place and the owner was about ready to sell the mother slave with her five small children. The children carried on so much because they were to be separated that the mistress bought them back although she had very little money to spare."

"I don't know any more slave stories, but now I am getting old, and I know that I do not have long to live, but I'm not sorry, I am, ready to go. I have lived as the Lord wants us to live and I know that when I die I shall join many of my friends and relatives in the Lord's place. Religion is the finest thing on earth. It is the one and only thing that matters."

Slave Narratives

Former Slave Interview, Special
Aug 16, 1937

Butler County, District #2
Middletown

MRS. NANCY EAST
809 Seventeenth Ave.,
Middletown, Ohio

NANCY EAST

"Mammy" East, 809 Seventeenth Ave., Middletown, Ohio, rules a four-room bungalow in the negro district set aside by the American Rolling Mill Corporation. She lives there with her sons, workers in the mill, and keeps them an immaculate home in the manner which she was taught on a Southern plantation. Her house is furnished with modern electrical appliances and furniture, but she herself is an anachronism, a personage with no faith in modern methods of living, one who belongs in that vague period designated as "befo' de wah."

"I 'membahs all 'bout de slave time. I was powerful small but my mother and daddy done tole me all 'bout it. Mother and daddy bofe come from Vaginny; mother's mama did too. She was a weaver and made all our clothes and de white folks clothes. Dat's all she ever did; just weave and spin. Gran'mama and her chilluns was sold to the Lett fambly, two brothers from Monroe County, Alabama. Sole jist like cows, honey, right off the block, jist like cows. But they was good to they slaves.

"My mother's last name was Lett, after the white folks, and my daddy's name was Harris Mosley, after his master. After mother and daddy married, the Mosleys done bought her from the Letts so they could be together. They was brother-in-laws. Den I was named after Miss Nancy. Dey was Miss Nancy and Miss Hattie and two boys in the Mosleys. Land, honey, they had a big (waving her hands in the air) plantation; a whole section; and de biggest home you done ever see. We darkies had cabins. Jist as clean and nice. Them Mosleys, they had a grist mill and a gin. They like my daddy and he worked in de mill for them. Dey sure was good to us. My mother worked on de place for Miss Nancy."

Mammy East, in a neat, voile dress and little pig-tails all over her head, is a tall, light-skinned Negro, who admits that she would much rather care for children than attend to the other duties of the little house she owns; but the white spreads on the beds and the spotless kitchen is no indication of this fact. She has a passion for the good old times when the Negroes had security with no responsibility. Her tall, statuesque appearance is in direct contrast to the present-day conception of old southern "mammmies."

"De wah, honey? Why, when dem Yankees come through our county mother and Miss Nancy and de rest hid de hosses in de swamps and hid other things in the house, but dey got all the cattle and hogs. Killed 'em, but only took the hams. Killed all de chickens and things, too. But dey didn't hurt the house.

"After de wah, everybody jist went on working same as ever. Then one day a white mans come riding through the county and tole us we was free. Free! Honey, did yo' hear that? Why we always had been free. He didn't know what he was talking 'bout. He kept telling us we was free and dat we oughtn't to work for no white folks 'less'n we got paid for it. Well Miss Nancy took care of us then. We got our cabin and a piece of ground for a garden and a share of de crops. Daddy worked in de mill. Miss Nancy saw to it that we always had nice clothes too.

"Ku Klux, honey? Why, we nevah did hear tell of no sich thing where we was. Nevah heered nothin' 'bout dat atall until we come up here, and dey had em here. Law, honey, folks don't know when dey's well off. My daddy worked in de mill and save his money, and twelve yeahs aftah de wah he bought two hundred and twenty acres of land, 'bout ten miles away. Den latah on daddy bought de mill from de Mosleys too. Yas'm, my daddy was well off.

"My, you had to be somebody to votes. I sure do 'membahs all 'bout dat. You had to be edicated and have money to votes. But I don' 'membahs no trouble 'bout de votin'. Not where we come from, no how.

"I was married down dere. Mah husband's fust name was Monroe after the county we lived in. My chilluns was named aftah some of the Mosleys. I got a Ed and Hattie. Aftah my daddy died we each got forty acahs. I sold mine and come up here to live with my boys.

"But honey dis ain't no way to raise chilluns. Not lak dey raised now. All dis dishonesty and stealin' and laziness. No mam! Look here at my gran'sons. Eatin' offen dey daddy. No place for 'em. Got edication, and caint git no jobs outside cuttin' grass and de like. Down on de plantation ev'body worked. No laziness er 'oneriness, er nothin! I tells yo' honey, I sure do wish these chilluns had de chances we had. Not much learnin', but we had up-bringin'! Look at dem chilluns across de street. Jist had a big fight ovah dere, and dey mothah's too lazy to do any thing 'bout it. No'm, nevah did see none o' dat when we was young. Gittin' in de folkeses hen houses and stealing, and de carryins on at night. No mam! I sure do wish de old times was here.

"I went back two-three yeahs ago, to de old home place, and dere it was, jist same as when I was livin' with Miss Nancy. Co'se, theys all dead and gone now, but some of the gran'chilluns was around. Yas'm, I membahs heap bout dem times."

Miriam Logan, Reporter
Lebanon, Ohio

Warren County, District 21

Story of WADE GLENN from Winston-Salem North Carolina:
(doesn't know his age)

WADE GLENN

"Yes Madam, I were a slave—I'm old enough to have been born into slavery, but I was only a baby slave, for I do not remember about slavery, I've just heard them tell about it. My Mammy were Lydia Glenn, and father were Caesar Glenn, for they belonged to old Glenn. I've heard tell he were a mean man too. My birthday is October 30th—but what year—I don't know. There were eight brothers and two sisters. We lived on John Beck's farm—a big farm, and the first work for me to do was picking up chips o' wood, and lookin' after hogs.

"In those days they'd all kinds of work by hand on the farm. No Madam, no cotton to speak of, or tobacco then. Just farmin' corn, hogs, wheat fruit,—like here. Yes Madam, that was all on John Beck's farm except the flax and the big wooley sheep. Plenty of nice clean flax-cloth suits we all had.

"Beck wasn't so good—but we had enough to eat, wear, and could have our Saturday afternoon to go to town, and Sunday for church. We sho did have church, large meetin'—camp meetin'—with lot of singin' an shoutin' and it was fine! Nevah was no singer, but I was a good dancer in my day, yes—yes Madam I were a good dancer. I went to dances and to church with my folks. My father played a violin. He played well, so did my brother, but I never did play or sing. Mammy sang a lot when she was spinning and weaving. She sing an' that big wheel a turnin.'

> "When I can read my title clear,
> Up Yonder, Up Yonder, Up Yonder!

and another of her spinnin' songs was a humin:—

> "The Promise of God Salvation free to give..."

"Besides helpin' on the farm, father was ferryman on the Yadkin River for Beck. He had a boat for hire. Sometimes passengers would want to go a mile, sometimes 30. Father died at thirty-five. He played the violin fine. My brother played for dances, and he used to sing lots of songs:—

> "Ol' Aunt Katy, fine ol' soul,
> She's beatin' her batter,
> In a brand new bowl...

—that was a fetchin' tune, but you see I can't even carry it. Maybe I could think up the words of a lot of those ol' tunes but they ought to pay well for them, for they make money out of them. I liked to go to church and to dances both. For a big church to sing I like 'Nearer My God to Thee'—there isn't anything so good for a big crowd to sing out big!

"Father died when he was thirty-five of typhoid. We all had to work hard. I came up here in 1892—and I don't know why I should have, for Winston-Salem was a big place. I've worked on farm and roads. My wife died ten years ago. We adopted a girl in Tennennesee years ago, and she takes a care of me now. She was always good to us—a good girl. Yes, Madam."

Wade Glenn proved to be not nearly so interesting as his appearance promised. He is short; wears gold rimmed glasses; a Southern Colonel's Mustache and Goatee— and capitals are need to describe the style! He had his comical-serious little countenance topped off with a soft felt hat worn at the most rakish angle. He can't carry a tune, and really is not musical. His adopted daughter with whom he lives is rated the town's best colored cook.

United States. Work Projects Administration

Ohio Guide, Special
Ex-Slave Stories
August 16, 1937

DAVID A. HALL

DAVID A. HALL

"I was born at Goldsboro, N.C., July 25, 1847. I never knew who owned my father, but my mother's master's name was Lifich Pamer. My mother did not live on the plantation but had a little cabin in town. You see, she worked as a cook in the hotel and her master wanted her to live close to her work. I was born in the cabin in town.

"No, I never went to school, but I was taught a little by my master's daughter, and can read and write a little. As a slave boy I had to work in the military school in Goldsboro. I waited on tables and washed dishes, but my wages went to my master the sane as my mother's.

"I was about fourteen when the war broke out, and remember when the Yankees came through our town. There was a Yankee soldier by the name of Kuhns who took charge of a Government Store. He would sell tobacco and such like to the soldiers. He was the man who told me I was free and then give me a job working in the store.

"I had some brothers and sisters but I do not remember them—can't tell you anything about them.

"Our beds were homemade out of poplar lumber and we slept on straw ticks. We had good things to eat and a lot of corn cakes and sweet potatoes. I had pretty good clothes, shoes, pants and a shirt, the same winter and summer.

"I don't know anything about the plantation as I had to work in town and did not go out there very much. No, I don't know how big it was or how many slaves there was. I never heard of any uprisings either.

"Our overseer was 'poor white-trash', hired by the master. I remember the master lived in a big white house and he was always kind to his slaves, so was his wife and children, but we didn't like the overseer. I heard of some slaves being whipped, but I never was and I did not see any of the others get punished. Yes, there was a jail on the plantation where slaves had to go if they wouldn't behave. I never saw a slave in chains but I have seen colored men in the chain gang since the war.

"We had a negro church in town and slaves that could be trusted could go to church. It was a Methodist Church and we sang negro spirituals.

"We could go to the funeral of a relative and quit work until it was over and then went back to work. There was a graveyard on the plantation.

"A lot of slaves ran away and if they were caught they were brought back and put in the stocks until they were sold. The master would never keep a runaway slave. We used to have fights with the 'white trash' sometimes and once I was hit by a rock throwed by a white boy and that's what this lump on my head is.

"Yes, we had to work every day but Sunday. The slaves did not have any holidays. I did not have time to play games but used to watch the slaves sing and dance after dark. I don't remember any stories.

"When the slaves heard they had been set free, I remember a lot of them were sorry and did not want to leave the plantation. No, I never heard of any in our section getting any mules or land.

"I do remember the 'night riders' that come through our country after the war. They put the horse shoes on the horses backwards and wrapped the horses feet in burlap so we couldn't hear them coming. The colored folks were deathly afraid of these men and would all run and hide when they heard they were coming. These 'night riders' used to steal everything the colored people had—even their beds and straw ticks.

"Right after the war I was brought north by Mr. Kuhns I spoke of, and for a short while I worked at the milling trade in Tiffin and came to Canton in 1866. Mr. Kuhns owned a part in the old flour mill here (now the Ohio Builders and Milling Co.) and he give me a job as a miller. I worked there until the end of last year, 70 years, and I am sure this is a record in Canton. No, I never worked any other place.

"I was married July 4, 1871 to Jennie Scott in Massillon. We had four children but they are all dead except one boy. Our first baby—a girl named Mary Jane, born February 21, 1872, was the first colored child born in Canton. My wife died in 1926. No, I do not know when she was born, but I do know she was not a slave.

"I started to vote after I came north but did not ever vote in the south. I do not like the way the young people of today live; they are too fast and drink too much. Yes, I think this is true of the white children the same as the colored.

"I saved my money when I worked and when I quit I had three properties. I sold one of these, gave one to my son, and I am living in the other. No, I have never had to ask for charity. I also get a pension check from, the mill where I worked so long.

"I joined church simply because I thought it would make me a better man and I think every one should belong. I have been a member of St. Paul's A.M.E. church here in Canton for 54 years. Yesterday (Sunday, August 15, 1937) our church celebrated by burning the mortgage. As I was the oldest member I was one of the three who lit it, the other two are the only living charter members. My church friends made me a present yesterday of $100.00 which was a birthday gift. I was 90 years old the 25th of last month."

Hall resides at 1225 High Ave., S.W., Canton, Ohio.

Miriam Logan
Lebanon, Ohio

MRS. CELIA HENDERSON, aged 88
Born Hardin County, Kentucky in 1849

(drawing of Celia Henderson) [TR: no drawing found]

CELIA HENDERSON

"Mah mammy were Julia Dittoe, an pappy, he were name Willis Dittoe. Dey live at Louieville till mammy were sold fo' her marster's debt. She were a powerful good cook, mammy were—an she were sol' fo to pay dat debt."

"She tuk us four chillen 'long wid her, an pappy an th' others staid back in Louieville. Dey tuk us all on a boat de Big Ribber—evah heah ob de big ribber? Mississippi its name—but we calls it de big ribber."

"Natchez on de hill—dats whaah de tuk us to. Nactchez-on-de-hill dis side of N' Or'leans. Mammy she have eleven chillen. No 'em, don't 'member all dem names no mo'. No 'em, nevah see pappy no moah. Im 'member mammy cryin' goin' down on de boat, and us chillen a cryin' too, but de place we got us was a nice place, nicer den what we left. Family 'o name of GROHAGEN it was dat got us. Yas'em dey was nice to mammy fo' she was a fine cook, mammy wus. A fine cook!"

"Me? Go'Long! I ain't no sech cook as my mammy was. But mah boy, he were a fine cook. I ain't nothin' of a cook. Yas'em, I cook fo Mis Gallagher, an fo 4 o' de sheriffs here, up at de jail. But de fancy cookin' I ain't much on, no'em I ain't. But mah boy an mammy now, dey was fine! Mah boy cook at hotels and wealthy homes in Louieville 'til he died."

"Dey was cotton down dere in Natchez, but no tobacco like up here. No 'em, I nevah wuk in cotton fields. I he'p mammy tote water, hunt chips, hunt pigs, get things outa de col' house. Dat way, I guess I went to wuk when I wuz about 7 or 8 yeahs ol'. Chillen is sma't now, an dey hafto be taught to wuk, but dem days us culled chillen wuk; an we had a good time wukin' fo dey wernt no shows, no playthings lak dey have now to takey up day time, no'em."

"Nevah no church fo' culled people does I 'member in Natchez. One time dey was a drouth, an de water we hauls from way ovah to de rivah. Now dat wuz down right wuk, a haulin dat water. Dey wuz an ol' man, he were powerful in prayer, an gather de darkies unda a big tree, an we all kneels down whilse he pray fo de po' beastes what needs good clean water fo to drink. Dat wuz a putty sight, dat church meetin' under de big tree. I alus member dat, an how, dat day he foun a spring wid he ol' cane, jes' like a miracle after prayer. It were a putty sight to see mah cows an all de cattle a trottin' fo dat water. De mens dey dug out a round pond fo' de water to run up into outa de spring, an it wuz good watah dat wudn't make de beastes sick, an we-all was sho' happy.'"

"Yes'em, I'se de only one of mammy's chillen livin'. She had 11 chillen. Mah gran'na on pappy's side, she live to be one hundred an ten yeah's ol' powerful ol' ev'y body say, an she were part Indian, gran'ma were, an dat made her live to be ol'.

"Me? I had two husband an three chillen. Mah firs' husban die an lef' me wid three little chillens, an mah secon' husban', he die 'bout six yeahs ago. Ah cum heah to Lebanon about forty yeahs ago, because mah mammy were heah, an she wanted me to come. When ah wuz little, we live nine yeahs in Natchez on de hill. Den when de wah were ovah Mammy she want to go back to Louieville fo her folks wuz all theah. Ah live in Louieville til ah cum to Lebanon. All ah 'members bout de close o' de wah, wuz dat white folks wuz broke up an po' down dere at Natchez; and de fus time ah hears de EMANICAPTION read out dey was a lot o' prancin 'roun, an a big time."

"Ah seen soldiers in blue down there in Natchez on de hill, oncet ah seen dem cumin down de road when ah were drivin mah cows up de road. Ah wuz scared sho, an' ah hid in de bushes side o' de road til dey went by, don' member dat mah cows was much scared though." Mammy say 'bettah hide when you sees sojers a-marchin by, so dat time a whole line o dem cum along and I hide."

"Down dere mammy done her cookin' outa doors, wid a big oven. Yo gits yo fiah goin' jes so under de oven, den you shovels some fiah up on top de oven fo to get you bakin jes right. Dey wuz big black kettles wid hooks an dey run up an down like on pulleys ovah de oven stove. Den dere wuz de col'house. No 'lectric ice box lak now, but a house under groun' wheah things wuz kept jest as col' as a ice box. No'em don't 'member jes how it were fix inside."

"Yas'em we comes back to Louieville. Yes'em mah

chillen goes to school, lak ah nevah did. Culled teachers in de culled school. Yes'em mah chillen went far as dey could take 'em."

"Medicin? My ol' mammy were great fo herb doctorin' an I holds by dat too a good deal, yas'em. Now-a-days you gets a rusty nail in yo foot an has lockjaw. But ah member mammy—she put soot mix wid bacon fryin's on mah foot when ah run a big nail inter it, an mah foot get well as nice!"

"Long time ago ah cum heah to see mammy, Ah got a terrible misery. Ah wuz asleep a dreamin bout it, an a sayin, "Mammy yo reckon axel grease goin' to he'p it?" Den ah wake up an go to her wheahs she's sleepin an say it.

"What fo axel grease gointo hep?—an I tol her, an she say:—

"Axel grease put on hot, wid red flannel goin'to tak it away chile."

Ah were an ol' woman mahse'f den—bout fifty, but mammy she climb outa bed an go out in de yard where deys an ol' wagon, an she scrapes dat axel off, an heat it up an put it on wid red flannel. Den ah got easy! Ah sho was thankful when dat grease an flannel got to wukin on me!

"You try it sometime when you gets one o' dem col' miseries in de winter time. But go 'long! Folks is too sma't nowadays to use dem good ol' medicines. Dey jes' calls de Doctor an he come an cut 'em wide open fo de 'pendycitus—he sho do! Yas'em ah has de doctor, ef ah needs him. Ah has de rheumatism, no pain—ah jes gets stiffer, an' stiffer right along."

Mah sight sho am poor now. Ah cain't wuk no mo. Ah done ironin aftah ah quit cookin—washin an ironin, ah likes a nice wash an iron the bes fo wuk. But lasyear mah eyes done give out on me, an dey tell me not to worry dey gointo give me a pension. De man goes to a heap o' wuk to get dem papers fix jes right."

"Yes 'em, I'se de on'y one o' mammy's chillen livin. Mah, gran'ma on pappy's side, she live to be one hundred and ten yeah's ol—powerful ol eve'ybody say. She were part Indian, gran' ma were, an dat made her to be ol."

"Yes'em, mos' I evah earn were five dollars a week. Ah gets twenty dollars now, an pays eight dollars fo rent. We is got no mo'—ah figgers—a wukin fo ourself den what we'd have wuz we slaves, fo dey gives you a log house, an clothes, an yo eats all yo want to, an when you buys things, maybe you doesn't make enough to git you what you needs, wukin sun-up to sun down. No' em 'course ah isn't wukin now when you gits be de hour—wukin people does now; but ah don't know nothin 'but that way o'doin."

"We weahs cotton cloths when ah were young, jes plain weave it were; no collar nor cuffs, n' belt like store clothes. Den men's jes have a kinda clothes like ... well, like a chemise, den some pantaloons wid a string run through at de knees. Bare feet—yes'em, no shoes. Nevah need no coat down to Natchez, no'em."

"When we comes back to Louieville on de boat, we sleeps in de straw on de flo' o' de boat. It gits colder 'n colder! Come big chunks ol ice down de river. De sky am dark, an hit col' an spit snow. Ah wish ah were back dere in Natchez dat time after de war were ovah! Yes'em, ah members dat much."

"Ah wuk along wid mammy til ah were married, den ah gits on by mahsef. Manny she come heah to Lebanon wid de Suttons—she married Sam. Sutton's pappy. Yes 'em dey wuz about 12 o'de fambly cum heah, an ah come to see mammy,... den ah gits me wuk, an ah stays.

"Cookin'? Yes'em, way meat is so high now, ah likes groundhog. Ground hog is good eatin. A peddler was by wid groun' hog fo ten cents apiece. Ground hog is good as fried chicken any day. You cleans de hog, an boils it in salt water til its tender. Den you makes flour gravy, puts it on after de water am drain off; you puts it in de oven wif de lid on an bakes hit a nice brown. No 'em, don' like fish so well, nor coon, nor possum, dey is too greasy. Likes chicken, groundhog an pork." Wid de wild meat you wants plain boiled potatoes, yes'em Irish potatoes, sho enough, ah heard o' eatin skunk, and muskrat, but ah ain't cookin em. But ah tells you dat groun' hog is good eatin.

"Ah were Baptized by a white minister in Louieville, an' ah been a Baptist fo' sixty yeahs now. Yes'em dey is plenty o' colored churches in Louisville now, but when I were young, de white folks has to see to it dat we is Baptised an knows Bible verses an' hymns. Dere want no smart culled preachers like Reverend Williams ... an dey ain't so many now."

"Up to Xenia is de culled school, an dey is mo's smart culled folks, ol' ones too—dat could give you-all a real story if you finds dem. But me, ah cain't read, nor write, and don't member's nuthin fo de War no good."

Celia is very black as to complexion; tall spare; has small grey eyes. In three long interviews she has tried very hard to remember for us from her youth and back through the years; it seems to trouble her that she cannot remember more. Samuel Sutton's father married her mother. Neither she or Samuel had the kind of a story to tell that I was expecting to hear from what little I know about colored people. I may have tried to get them on the songs and amusements of their youth too often, but it seems that most that they knew was work; did not sing or have a very good time. Of course I thought they would say that slavery was terrible, but was surprised there too. Colored people here are used to having white people come for them to work as they have no telephones, and most white people only hire colored help by the day or as needed. Celia and Samuel, old age pensioners, were very apoligetic because they are no longer able to work.

United States. Work Projects Administration

WPA in Ohio
Federal Writers' Project
Bishop & Isleman
Reporter: Bishop
[HW: Revised]

Topic: Ex-Slaves.
Jefferson County, District #5
July 6, 1937

GEORGE JACKSON
Ex-Slave, 79 years

GEORGE JACKSON

I was born in Loudon County, Virginny, Feb. 6, 1858. My mother's name was Betsy Jackson. My father's name was Henry Jackson. Dey were slaves and was born right der in Loudon County. I had 16 brothers and sisters. All of dem is dead. My brothers were Henry, Richard, Wesley, John and me; Sisters were Annie, Marion, Sarah Jane, Elizabeth, Alice, Cecila and Meryl. Der were three other chillun dat died when babies.

I can remember Henry pullin' me out of de fire. I've got scars on my leg yet. He was sold out of de family to a man dat was Wesley McGuest. Afterwards my brother was taken sick with small-pox and died.

We lived on a big plantation right close to Bloomfield, Virginny. I was born in de storeroom close to massa's home. It was called de weavin' room—place where dey weaved cotton and yarn. My bed was like a little cradle bed and dey push it under de big bed at day time.

My grandfather died so my mother told me, when he was very old. My grandmother died when se bout 96. She went blind fore she died. Dey were all slaves.

My father was owned by John Butler and my grandmother was owned by Tommy Humphries. Dey were both farmers. My massa joined de war. He was killed right der where he lived.

When my father wanted to cum home he had to get a permit from his massa. He would only cum home on Saturday. He worked on de next plantation joinin' us. All us chillun and my mother belonged to Massa Humphries.

I worked in de garden, hoein' weeds and den I washed dishes in de kitchen. I never got any money.

I eat fat pork, corn bread, black molasses and bad milk. The meat was mostly boiled. I lived on fat meat and corn bread. I don't remember eatin' rabbit, possum or fish.

De slaves on our plantation did not own der own garden. Dey ate vegetables out of de big garden.

In hot weather I wore gean pants and shirt. De pants were red color and shirt white. I wore heavy woolen clothes in de winter. I wore little britches wid jacket fastened on. I went barefooted in de summer.

De mistress scold and beat me when I was pullin' weeds. Sometimes I pulled a cabbage stead of weed. She would jump me and beat me. I can remember cryin'. She told me she had to learn me to be careful. I remember the massa when he went to war. He was a picket in an apple tree. A Yankee soldier spied and shot him out of de tree.

I remember Miss Ledig Humphries. She was a pretty girl and she had a sister Susie. She married a Mr. Chamlain who was overseer. Der were Robert and Herbert Humphries. Dey were older dan me. Robert wuz about 15 years old when de war surrender.

De one that married Susie was de overseer. He was pretty rough. I don't remember any white neighbors round at dat time.

Der were 450 acres of de plantation. I can't remember all de slaves. I know der were 80, odd slaves.

Lots of mornings I would go out hours fore daylight and when it was cold my feet would 'most freeze. They all knew dey had to get up in de mornin'. De slaves all worked hard and late at night.

I heerd some say that the overseer would take dem to de barn. I remember Tom Lewis. Then his massa sold him to our massa he told him not to let the overseer whip him. The overseer said he would whip him. One day Tom did something wrong. The overseer ordered him to de barn. Tom took his shirt off to get ready for de whippin' and when de overseer raised de whip Tom gave him one lick wid his fist and broke de overseer's neck.

Den de massa sold Tom to a man by de name of Joseph Fletcher. He stayed with old man Fletcher til he died.

Fore de slaves were sold dey were put in a cell place til next day when dey would be sold. Uncle Marshall and Douglas were sold and I remember dem handcuffed but I never saw dem on de auction block.

I never knew nothin' bout de Bible til after I was free.

I went to school bout three months. I was 19 or 20 years old den.

My uncle Bill heard dey were goin' to sell him and he run away. He went north and cum back after de surrender. He died in Bluemont, Virginny, bout four years ago.

After de days work dey would have banjo pickin', singin' and dancin'. Dey work all day Saturday and Saturday night those dat had wives to see would go to see dem. On Sunday de would sit around.

When Massa was shot my mother and dem was cryin'.

When Slaves were sick one of the mammies would look after dem and dey would call de doctor if she couldn't fix de sick.

I remember de big battle dey fought for four days on de plantation. That was de battle of Bull Run. I heard shootin' and saw soldiers shot down. It was one of de worst fights of de war. It was right between Blue Ridge and Bull Run mountain. De smoke from de shootin' was just like a fog. I saw horses and men runnin' to de fight and men shot off de horses. I heard de cannon roar and saw de locust tree cut off in de yard. Some of de bullets smashed de house. De apple tree where my massa was shot from was in de orchard not far from de house.

De Union Soldiers won de battle and dey camped right by de house. Dey helped demselves to de chickens and cut their heads off wid their swords. Dey broke into de cellar and took wine and preserves.

After de war I worked in de cornfield. Dey pay my

mother for me in food and clothes. But dey paid my mother money for workin' in de kitchen.

De slaves were awful glad bout de surrender.

De Klu Klux Klan, we called dem de paroles, dey would run de colored people, who were out late, back home. I know no school or church or land for negroes. I married in Farguar [HW: Farquhar] Co., state of Virginny, in de county seat. Dat was in 1883. I was married by a Methodist preacher in Leesburg. I did not get drunk, but had plenty to drink. We had singin' and music. My sister was a religious woman and would not allow dancin'.

I have fourteen chillun. Four boys are livin' and two girls. All are married. George, my oldest boy graduated from grade school and de next boy. I have 24 grandchillun and one great grandson. John, my son is sickly and not able to work and my daughter, Mamie has nine chillun to support. Her husband doesn't have steady work.

The grandchillun are doin' pretty well.

I think Abraham Lincoln was a fine man. It was put in his mind to free de colored people. Booker T. Washington was alright.

Henry Logan, a colored man that lives near Bridgeport, Ohio is a great man. He is a deacon in de Mt. Zion Baptist church. He is a plasterer and liked by de colored and white people.

I think it wuz a fine thing that slavery was finished. I don't have a thing more than my chillun and dey are all poor. (A grandchild nearby said, "We are as poor as church mice".) My chillun are my best friends and dey love me.

I first joined church at Upperville, Virginny. I was buried under de water. I feel dat everybody should have religion. Dey get on better in dis life, and not only in dis life but in de life to cum.

My overseer wuz just a plain man. He wasn't hard. I worked for him since the surrender and since I been a man. I was down home bout six yares ago and met de overseer's son and he took me and my wife around in his automobile.

My wife died de ninth of last October (1936). I buried her in Week's cemetery, near Bridgeport, Ohio. We have a family burial lot there. Dat where I want to be buried, if I die around here.

• Description Of George Jackson
[TR: original "Word Picture" struck out]

George Jackson is about 5 feet 6 inches tall and weighs 145 lbs. He has not done any manual labor for the past two years. He attends church regularly at the Mt. Zion Baptist church. As he only attended school about four months his reading is limited. His vision and hearing is fair and he takes a walk everyday. He does not smoke, chew or drink intoxicating beverages.

His wife, Malina died October 9, 1936 and was buried at Bridgeport, Ohio. He lives with his daughter-in-law whose husband forks for a junk dealer. The four room house that they rent for $20 per month is in a bad state of repairs and is in the midst of one of the poorest sections of Steubenville.

United States. Work Projects Administration

WPA in Ohio
Federal Writers' Project
Written by Bishop & Isleman
Edited by Albert I. Dugen [TR: also reported as Dugan]

Ex-Slaves
Jefferson County, District #2
PERRY SID JEMISON [TR: also reported as Jamison]
Ex-Slave, 79 years

PERRY SID JEMISON

"I wuz borned in Perry County, Alabama! De way I remember my age is, I was 37 years when I wuz married and dat wuz 42 years ago the 12th day of last May. I hed all dis down on papers, but I hab been stayin' in different places de last six years and lost my papers and some heavy insurance in jumpin' round from place to place.

"My mudders name wuz Jane Perry. Father's name wuz Sid Jemison. Father died and William Perry was mudders second husband.

"My mudder wuz a Virginian and my father was a South Carolinian. My oldest brodder was named Sebron and oldest sister wuz Maggie. Den de next brudder wuz William, de next sister wuz named Artie, next Susie. Dats all of dem.

"De hol entire family lived together on the Cakhoba river, Perry County, Alabama. After dat we wuz scattered about, some God knows where.

"We chillun played 'chicken me craner crow'. We go

out in de sand and build sand houses and put out little tools and one thing and another in der.

"When we wuz all together we lived in a log hut. Der wuz a porch in between and two rooms on each side. De porch wuz covered over—all of it wuz under one roof.

"Our bed wuz a wooden frame wid slats nailed on it. We jus had a common hay mattress to sleep on. We had very respectable quilts, because my mudder made them. I believe we had better bed covers dem days den we hab des days.

"My grandmother wuz named Snooky and my grandfather Anthony. I thought der wasn't a better friend in all de world den my grandmother. She would do all she could for her grandchildren. Der wuz no food allowance for chillun that could not work and my grandmother fed us out of her and my mudders allowance. I member my grandmudder giving us pot-licker, bread and red syrup.

"De furst work I done to get my food wuz to carry water in de field to de hands dat wuz workin'. De next work after dat, wuz when I wuz large enough to plow. Den I done eberything else that come to mind on de farm. I neber earned money in dem slave days.

"Your general food wuz such as sweet potatoes, peas and turnip greens. Den we would jump out and ketch a coon or possum. We ate rabbits, squirrels, ground-hog and hog meat. We had fish, cat-fish and scale fish. Such things as greens, we boil dem. Fish we fry. Possum we parboil den pick him up and bake him. Of all dat meat I prefar fish and rabbit. When it come to vegetables, cabbage wuz my delight, and turnips. De slaves had their own garden patch.

"I wore one piece suit until I wuz near grown, jes one garment dat we called et dat time, going out in your shirt tail. In de winter we had cotton shirt with a string to tie de collar, instead of a button and tie. We war den same on Sunday, excepting dat mudder would wash and iron dem for dat day.

"We went barefooted in de summer and in de winter we wore brogan shoes. Dey were made of heavy stiff leather.

"My massa wuz named Sam Jemison and his wife wuz named Chloe. Dey had chillun. One of the boys wuz named Sam after his father. De udder wuz Jack. Der wuz daughter Nellie. Dem wuz all I know bout. De had a large six room building. It wuz weather boarded and built on de common order.

"Dey hed 750 acres on de plantation. De Jemisons sold de plantation to my uncle after the surrender and I heard him say ever so many times that it was 750 acres. Der wuz bout 60 slaves on de plantation. Dey work hard and late at night. Dey tole me dey were up fore daylight and in de fields til dark.

"I heard my mudder say dat the mistress was a fine woman, but dat de marse was rigied [TR: rigid?].

"De white folks did not help us to learn to read or write. De furst school I remember dat wuz accessbile was foh 90 days duration. I could only go when it wuz too wet to work in de fields. I wuz bout 16 years when I went to de school.

"Der wuz no church on de plantation. Couldn't none of us read. But after de surrender I remember de furst preacher I ebber heard. I remember de text. His name was Charles Fletcher. De text was "Awake thou dat sleepeth, arise from de dead and Christ will give you life!" I remember of one of de baptizing. De men dat did it was Emanuel Sanders. Dis wuz de song dat dey sing: "Beside de gospel pool, Appointed for de poor." Dat is all I member of dat song now.

"I heard of de slaves running away to de north, but I nebber knew one to do it. My mudder tole me bout patrollers. Dey would ketch de slaves when dey were out late and whip and thress dem. Some of de owners would not stand for it and if de slaves would tell de massa he might whip de patrollers if he could ketch dem.

"I knowed one colored boy. He wuz a fighter. He wuz six foot tall and over 200 pounds. He would not stand to be whipped by de white man. Dey called him Jack. Des wuz after de surrender. De white men could do nothin' wid him. En so one day dey got a crowd together and dey shoot him. It wuz a senation [TR: sensation?] in de country, but no one was arrested for it.

"De slaves work on Saturday afternoon and sometimes on Sunday. On Saturday night de slaves would slip around to de next plantation and have parties and dancin' and so on.

"When I wuz a child I played, 'chicken me craner crow' and would build little sand houses and call dem frog dens and we play hidin' switches. One of de play songs wuz 'Rockaby Miss Susie girl' and 'Sugar Queen in goin south, carrying de young ones in her mouth.'

"I remember several riddles. One wuz:

> 'My father had a little seal,
> Sixteen inches high.
> He roamed the hills in old Kentuck,
> And also in sunny Spain.
> If any man can beat dat,
> I'll try my hand agin.'

"One little speech I know:

> 'I tumbled down one day,
> When de water was wide and deep
> I place my foot on the de goose's back
> And lovely swam de creek.'

"When I wuz a little boy I wuz follin' wid my father's scythe. It fell on my arm and nearly cut if off. Dey got somethin' and bind it up. Eventually after a while, it mended up.

"De marse give de sick slaves a dose of turpentine, blue mass, caromel and number six.

"After de surrender my mother tole me dat the marse told de slaves dat dey could buy de place or dey could share de crops wid him and he would rent dem de land.

"I married Lizzie Perry, in Perry County Alabama. A preacher married us by the name of John Jemison. We just played around after de weddin' and hed a good time til bedtime come, and dat wuz very soon wid me.

"I am de father of seven chillun. Both daughters married and dey are housekeepers. I have 11 grandchillun.

Three of dem are full grown and married. One of dem has graduated from high school.

"Abraham Lincoln fixed it so de slaves could be free. He struck off de handcuffs and de ankle cuffs from de slaves. But how could I be free if I had to go back to my massa and beg for bread, clothes and shelter? It is up to everybody to work for freedom.

"I don't think dat Jefferson Davus wuz much in favor of liberality. I think dat Booker T. Washington wuz a man of de furst magnitude. When it come to de historiance I don't know much about dem, but according to what I red in dem, Fred Douglas, Christopher Hatton, Peter Salem, all of dem colored men—dey wuz great men. Christopher Hatton wuz de furst slave to dream of liberty and den shed his blood for it. De three of dem play a conspicuous part in de emancipation.

"I think it's a good thing dat slavery is ended, for God hadn't intended there to be no man a slave.

"My reason for joining de church is, de church is said to be de furst born, the general assembly of the living God. I joined it to be in the general assembly of God.

"We have had too much destructive religion. We need pure and undefiled religion. If we had dat religion, conditions would be de reverse of that dey are."

(**Note:** The worker who interviewed this old man was impressed with his deep religious nature and the manner in which there would crop out in his conversation the facile use of such words as eventually, general, accessible, etc. The interview also revealed that the old man had a knowledge of the scripture. He claims to be a preacher and during the conversation gave indications of the oratory that is peculiar to old style colored preachers.)

• Word Picture Of Perry Sid Jamison And His Home

[TR: also reported as Jemison]

Mr. Jamison is about 5'2" and weighs 130 pounds. Except for a slight limp, caused by a broken bone that did not heal, necessitating the use of a cane, he gets around in a lively manner. He takes a walk each morning and has a smile for everybody.

Mr. Jamison is an elder in the Second Baptist Church and possesses a deep religious nature. In his conversation there crops out the facile use of such words as "eventually", "general", "accessible", and the like. He has not been engaged in manual labor since 1907. Since then he has made his living as an evangelist for the colored Baptist church.

Mr. Jamison says he does not like to travel around without something more than a verbal word to certify who and what he is. He produced a certificate from the "Illinois Theological Seminary" awarding him the degree of Doctor of Divinity and dated December 15, 1933, and signed by Rev. Walter Pitty for the trustees and S. Billup, D.D., Ph.D. as the president. Another document was a minister's license issued by the Probate court of Jefferson county authorizing him to perform marriage ceremonies. He has his ordination certificate dated November 7, 1900, at Red Mountain Baptist Church, Sloss, Alabama, which certifies that he was ordained an elder of that church; it is signed by Dr. G.S. Smith, Moderator. Then he has two letters of recommendation from churches in Alabama and Chicago.

That Mr. Jamison is a vigerous preacher is attested by other ministers who say they never knew a man of his age to preach like he does.

Mr. Jamison lives with his daughter, Mrs. Elizabeth Cookes, whose husband is a WPA worker. Also living in the house is the daughter's son, employed as a laborer, and his wife. Between them all, a rent of $28.00 a month is paid for the house of six rooms. The house at 424 S. Seventh Street, Steubenville, is in a respectable part of the city and is of the type used by poorer classes of laborers.

Mr. Jamison's wife died June 4, 1928, and since then he has lived with his daughter. In his conversation he gives indication of a latent oratory easily called forth.

K. Osthimer, Author

Folklore: Stories From Ex-Slaves
Lucas County, Dist. 9
Toledo, Ohio

The Story of MRS. JULIA KING of Toledo, Ohio.

JULIA KING

Mrs. Julia King resides at 731 Oakwood Avenue, Toledo, Ohio. Although the records of the family births were destroyed by a fire years ago, Mrs. King places her age at about eighty years. Her husband, Albert King, who died two years ago, was the first Negro policeman employed on the Toledo police force. Mrs. King, whose hair is whitening with age, is a kind and motherly woman, small in stature, pleasing and quiet in conversation. She lives with her adopted daughter, Mrs. Elizabeth King Kimbrew, who works as an elevator operator at the Lasalle & Koch Co. Mrs. King walks with a limp and moves about with some difficulty. She was the first colored juvenile officer in Toledo, and worked for twenty years under Judges O'Donnell and Austin, the first three years as a volunteer without pay.

Before her marriage, Mrs. King was Julia Ward. She was born in Louisville, Kentucky. Her parents Samuel and Matilda Ward, were slaves. She had one sister, Mary Ward, a year and a half older than herself.

She related her story in her own way. "Mamma was keeping house. Papa paid the white people who owned them, for her time. He left before Momma did. He run away to Canada on the Underground Railroad.

"My mother's mistress—I don't remember her name—used to come and take Mary with her to market every day. The morning my mother ran away, her mistress decided she wouldn't take Mary with her to market. Mamma was glad, because she had almost made up her mind to go, even without Mary.

"Mamma went down to the boat. A man on the boat told Mamma not to answer the door for anybody, until he gave her the signal. The man was a Quaker, one of those people who says 'Thee' and 'Thou'. Mary kept on calling out the mistress's name and Mamma couldn't keep her still.

"When the boat docked, the man told Mamma he thought her master was about. He told Mamma to put a veil over her face, in case the master was coming. He told Mamma he would cut the master's heart out and give it to her, before he would ever let her be taken.

"She left the boat before reaching Canada, somewhere on the Underground Railroad—Detroit, I think—and a woman who took her in said: 'Come in, my child, you're safe now.' Then Mama met my father in Windsor. I think they were taken to Canada free.

"I don't remember anything about grandparents at all.

"Father was a cook.

"Mother's mistress was always good and kind to her.

"When I was born, mother's master said he was

worth three hundred dollars more. I don't know if he ever would have sold me.

"I think our home was on the plantation. We lived in a cabin and there must have been at least six or eight cabins.

"Uncle Simon, who boarded with me in later years, was a kind of overseer. Whenever he told his master the slaves did something wrong, the slaves were whipped, and Uncle Simon was whipped, too. I asked him why he should be whipped, he hadn't done anything wrong. But Uncle Simon said he guessed he needed it anyway.

"I think there was a jail on the plantation, because Mamma said if the slaves weren't in at a certain hour at night, the watchman would lock them up if he found them out after hours without a pass.

"Uncle Simon used to tell me slaves were not allowed to read and write. If you ever got caught reading or writing, the white folks would punish you. Uncle Simon said they were beaten with a leather strap cut into strips at the end.

"I think the colored folks had a church, because Mamma was always a Baptist. Only colored people went to the church.

"Mamma used to sing a song:

> "Don't you remember the promise that you made,
> To my old dying mother's request?
> That I never should be sold,
> Not for silver or for gold.
> While the sun rose from the East to the West?

"And it hadn't been a year,
The grass had not grown over her grave.
I was advertised for sale.
And I would have been in jail,
If I had not crossed the deep, dancing waves.

"I'm upon the Northern banks
And beneath the Lion's paw,
And he'll growl if you come near the shore.

"The slaves left the plantation because they were sold and their children were sold. Sometimes their masters were mean and cranky.

"The slaves used to get together in their cabins and tell one another the news in the evening. They visited, the same as anybody else. Evenings, Mamma did the washing and ironing and cooked for my father.

"When the slaves got sick, the other slaves generally looked after them. They had white doctors, who took care of the families, and they looked after the slaves, too, but the slaves looked after each other when they got sick.

"I remember in the Civil War, how the soldiers went away. I seen them all go to war. Lots of colored folks went. That was the time we were living in Detroit. The Negro people were tickled to death because it was to free the slaves.

"Mamma said the Ku Klux was against the Catholics, but not against the Negroes. The Nightriders would turn out at night. They were also called the Know-Nothings, that's what they always said. They were the same as the Nightriders. One night, the Nightriders in Louisville surrounded a block of buildings occupied by Catholic people. They permitted the women and children to exscape, but killed all the men. When they found out the men were putting on women's clothes, they killed everything, women and children, too. It was terrible. That must have been about eighty years ago, when I was a very little girl.

"There was no school for Negro children during slavery, but they have schools in Louisville, now, and they're doing fine.

"I had two little girls. One died when she was three years old, the other when she was thirteen. I had two children I adopted. One died just before she was to graduate from Scott High School.

"I think Lincoln was a grand man! He was the first president I heard of. Jeff Davis, I think he was tough. He was against the colored people. He was no friend of the colored people. Abe Lincoln was a real friend.

"I knew Booker T. Washington and his wife. I belonged to a society that his wife belonged to. I think it was called the National Federation of Colored Women's Clubs. I heard him speak here in Toledo. I think it was in the Methodist church. He wanted the colored people to educate themselves. Lots of them wanted to be teachers and doctors, but he wanted them to have farms. He wanted them to get an education and make something of themselves. All the prominent Negro women belonged to the Club. We met once a year. I went to quite a few cities where the meetings were held: Detroit, Cleveland, and Philadelphia.

"The only thing I had against Frederick Douglass was that he married a white woman. I never heard Douglass speak.

"I knew some others too. I think Paul Lawrence Dunbar was a fine young man. I heard him recite his poems. He visited with us right here several times.

"I knew Charles Cottrell, too. He was an engraver. There was a young fellow who went to Scott High. He was quite an artist; I can't remember his name. He was the one who did the fine picture of my daughter that hangs in the parlor.

"I think slavery is a terrible system. I think slavery is the cause of mixing. If people want to choose somebody, it should be their own color. Many masters had children from their Negro slaves, but the slaves weren't able to help themselves.

"I'm a member of the Third Baptist Church. None join unless they've been immersed. That's what I believe in. I don't believe in christening or pouring. When the bishop was here from Cleveland, I said I wanted to be immersed. He said, 'We'll take you under the water as far as you care to go.' I think the other churches are good, too. But I was born and raised a Baptist. Joining a church or not joining a church won't keep you out of heaven, but I think you should join a church."

(Interview, Thursday, June 10, 1937.)

Story and Photo by Frank M. Smith

Ex-Slaves
Mahoning County, Dist. #5
Youngstown, Ohio

The Story of MRS. ANGELINE LESTER, of Youngstown, Ohio.

ANGELINE LESTER

Mrs. Angeline Lester lives at 836 West Federal Street, on U.S. Route #422, in a very dilapidated one story structure, which once was a retail store room with an addition built on the rear at a different floor level.

Angeline lives alone and keeps her several cats and chickens in the house with her. She was born on the plantation of Mr. Womble, near Lumpkin, Stewart County, Georgia about 1847, the exact date not known to her, where she lived until she was about four years old. Then her father was sold to a Dr. Sales, near Brooksville, Georgia, and her mother and a sister two years younger were sold to John Grimrs[HW:?], who in turn gave them to his newly married daughter, the bride of Henry Fagen, and was taken to their plantation, near Benevolence, Randolph County, Georgia.

When the Civil War broke out, Angeline, her mother and sister were turned over to Robert Smith, who substituted for Henry Fagen, in the Confederate Army.

Angeline remembers the soldiers coming to the plantation, but any news about the war was kept from them. After the war a celebration was held in Benevolence, Georgia, and Angeline says it was here she first tasted a roasted piece of meat.

The following Sunday, the negroes were called to their master's house where they were told they were free, and those who wished, could go, and the others could stay and he would pay them a fair wage, but if they left they could take only the clothing on their back. Angeline said "We couldn't tote away much clothes, because we were only given one pair of shoes and two dresses a year."

Not long after the surrender Angeline said, "My father came and gathered us up and took us away and we worked for different white folks for money". As time went on, Angeline's father and mother passed away, and she married John Lester whom she has outlived.

Angeline enjoys good health considering her age and she devotes her time working "For De Laud". She says she has "Worked for De Laud in New Castle, Pennsylvania, and I's worked for De Laud in Akron". She also says "De Laud does not want me to smoke, or drink even tea or coffee, I must keep my strength to work for De Laud".

After having her picture taken she wanted to know what was to be done with it and when told it was to be sent to Columbus or maybe to Washington, D.C. she said "Lawsy me, if you had tol' me befo' I'd fixed up a bit."

United States. Work Projects Administration

Betty Lugabill, Reporter [TR: also reported as Lugabell]
Harold Pugh, Editor
R.S. Drum, Supervisor
Jun 9, 1937

Folklore: Ex-Slaves
Paulding Co., District 10

KISEY McKIMM
Ex-Slave, 83 years

KISEY MCKIMM

Ah was born in Bourbon county, sometime in 1853, in the state of Kaintucky where they raise fine horses and beautiful women. Me 'n my Mammy, Liza 'n Joe, all belonged to Marse Jacob Sandusky the richest man in de county. Pappy, he belonged to de Henry Young's who owned de plantation next to us.

Marse Jacob was good to his slaves, but his son, Clay was mean. Ah remembah once when he took mah Mammy out and whipped her cauz she forgot to put cake in his basket, when he went huntin'. But dat was de las' time, cauz de master heard of it and cussed him lak God has come down from Hebbin.

Besides doin' all de cookin' 'n she was de best in de county, mah Mammy had to help do de chores and milk fifteen cows. De shacks of all de slaves was set at de edge of a wood, an' Lawse, honey, us chillun used to had to go out 'n gatha' all de twigs 'n brush 'n sweep it jes' lak a floor.

Den de Massa used to go to de court house in Paris 'n buy sheep an' hogs. Den we use to help drive dem home. In de evenin' our Mammy took de old cloes of Mistress Mary 'n made cloes fo' us to wear. Pappy, he come ovah to see us every Sunday, through de summer, but in de winter, we would only see him maybe once a month.

De great day on de plantation, was Christmas when we all got a little present from de Master. De men slaves would cut a whole pile of wood fo' de fiah place 'n pile it on de porch. As long as de whole pile of wood lasted we didn't hab to work but when it was gone, our Christmas was ovah. Sometimes on Sunday afternoons, we would go to de Master's honey room 'n he would gib us sticks of candied honey, an' Lawd chile was dem good. I et so much once, ah got sick 'nough to die.

Our Master was what white folks call a "miser". I remembah one time, he hid $3,000, between de floor an' de ceilin', but when he went fur it, de rats had done chewed it all up into bits. He used to go to de stock auction, every Monday, 'n he didn't weah no stockings. He had a high silk hat, but it was tore so bad, dat he held de top n' bottom to-gether wid a silk neckerchief. One time when ah went wid him to drive de sheep home, ah heard some of de men wid kid gloves, call him a "hill-billy" 'n make fun of his clothes. But he said, "Don't look at de clothes, but look at de man".

One time, dey sent me down de road to fetch somethin' 'n I heerd a bunch of horses comin', ah jumped ovah de fence 'n hid behind de elderberry bushes, until dey passed, den ah ran home 'n tol' 'em what ah done seen. Pretty soon dey come to de house, 125 Union soldiers an' asked fo' something to eat. We all jumped roun' and fixed dem a dinnah, when dey finished, dey looked for Master, but he was hid. Dey was gentlemen 'n didn't botha or take nothin'. When de war was ovah de Master gave Mammy a house an' 160 acre farm, but when he died, his son Clay tole us to get out of de place or he'd burn de house an' us up in it, so we lef an' moved to Paris. After I was married 'n had two children, me an my man moved north an' I've been heah evah since.

United States. Work Projects Administration

WPA in Ohio
Federal Writers' Project
Bishop & Isleman
Reporter: Bishop
July 7, 1937

Topic: Ex-Slaves.
Jefferson County, District #5
[HW: Steubenville]

THOMAS McMILLAN, Ex-Slave
(Does not know age)

THOMAS MCMILLAN

I was borned in Monroe County, Alabam. I do not know de date. My father's name was Dave McMillan and my mothers name was Minda. Dey cum from Old Virginny and he was sold from der. We lived in a log house. De beds hed ropes instead of slats and de chillun slept on de floor.

Dey put us out in de garden to pick out weeds from de potatoes. We did not get any money. We eat bread, syrup and potatoes. It wuz cooked in pots and some was made in fire, like ash cakes. We hed possum lots of times and rabbit and squirrel. When dey go fishin' we hed fish to eat. I liked most anything they gave us to eat.

In de summer we wore white shirt and pants and de same in de winter. We wore brogans in de winter too.

De Massa name wuz John and his wife died before I know her. He hed a boy named John. He lived in a big house. He done de overseeing himself.

He hed lots of acres in his plantation and he hed a big gang of slaves. He hed a man to go and call de slaves up at 4 o'clock every morning. He was good to his slaves and did not work them so late at night. I heard some of de slaves on other plantations being punished, but our boss take good care of us.

Our Massa learn some of us to read and write, but some of de udder massas did not.

We hed church under a arbor. De preacher read de bible and he told us what to do to be saved. I 'member he lined us up on Jordan's bank and we sung behind him.

De partrollers watch de slaves who were out at night. If dey have a pass dey were alright. If not dey would get into it. De patrollers whip dem and carry dem home.

On Saturday afternoon dey wash de clothes and stay around. On Sunday dey go to church. On Christmas day we did not work and dey make a nice meal for us. We sometimes shuck corn at night. We pick cotton plenty.

When we were chillun me other brudders and five sisters played marbles together.

I saw de blue jackets, dat's what we called de Yankee soldiers. When we heard of our freedom we hated it because we did not know what it was for and did not know where to go. De massa say we could stay as long as we pleased.

De Yankee soldier asked my father what dey wuz all doing around der and that dey were free. But we did not know where to go. We stayed on wid de massa for a long time after de war wuz over.

De Klu Klux Klan wuz pretty rough to us and dey whip us. Der was no school for us colored people.

I wuz nearly 20 when I first took up with my first woman and lived with her 20 years den I marry my present wife. I married her in Alabama and Elder Worthy wuz de preacher. We had seven chillun, all grandchillun are dead. I don't know where dey all are at excepting me daughter in Steubenville and she is a widow. She been keepin' rooms and wash a little for her living.

I didn't hear much bout de politics but I think Abraham Lincoln done pretty well. I reckon Jefferson Davis did the best he knowed how. Booker T. Washington, I nebber seen him, but he wuz a great man.

Religion is all right; can't find no fault with religion. I think all of us ought to be religious because the dear Lord died for us all. Dis world would be a better place if we all were religious.

• Word Picture of MR. MCMILLAN

Thomas McMillan, 909 Morris Ave., Steubenville, Ohio. He lives with his wife, Toby who is over 50 years old. He makes his living using a hand cart to collect junk. He is 5'6" tall and weighs 155 pounds. His beard is gray and hair white and close cropped. He attends Mt. Zion Baptist Church and lives his religion. He is able to read a little and takes pleasure in reading the bible and newspaper.

He has seven children. He has not heard of them for several years except one daughter who lives in Steubenville and is a widow.

His home is a three room shack and his landlord

lets him stay there rent free. The houses in the general surrounding are in a run down condition.

Wilbur Ammon, Editor
George Conn, Writer
C.R. McLean, District Supervisor
June 16, 1937

Folklore
Summit County, District #9

SARAH MANN

Mrs. Mann places her birth sometime in 1861 during the first year of the Civil War, on a plantation owned by Dick Belcher, about thirty miles southwest of Richmond, Virginia.

Her father, Frederick Green, was owned by Belcher and her mother, Mandy Booker, by Race Booker on an adjoining plantation. Her grandparents were slaves of Race Booker.

After the slaves were freed she went with her parents to Clover Hill, a small hamlet, where she worked out as a servant until she married Beverly Mann. Rev. Mike Vason, a white minister, performed the ceremony with, only her parents and a few friends present. At the close of the ceremony, the preacher asked if they would "live together as Isaac and Rebecca did." Upon receiving a satisfactory reply, he pronounced them man and wife.

Mr. and Mrs. Mann were of a party of more than 100 ex-slaves who left Richmond in 1880 for Silver Creek where Mr. Mann worked in the coal mines. Two years later they moved to Wadsworth where their first child was born.

In 1883 they came to Akron. Mr. Mann, working as laborer, was able to purchase two houses on Furnace Street, the oldest and now one of the poorer negro sections of the city. It is situated on a high bluff overlooking the Little Cuyahoga River.

Today Mrs. Mann, her daughter, a son-in-law and one grandchild occupy one of the houses. Three children were born to Mr. and Mrs. Mann, but only one is living. Mr. Mann, a deacon in the church, died three years ago. Time has laid its heavy hand on her property. It is the average home of colored people living in this section, two stories, small front yeard, enclosed with wooden picket fence. A large coal stove in front room furnishes heat. In recent years electricity has supplanted the overhead oil lamp.

Most of the furnishings were purchased in early married life. They are somewhat worn but arranged in orderly manner and are clean.

Mrs. Mann is tall and angular. Her hair is streaked with gray, her face thin, with eyes and cheek bones dominating. With little or no southern accent, she speaks freely of her family, but refrains from discussing affairs of others of her race.

She is a firm believer in the Bible. It is apparent she strives to lead a religious life according to her understanding. She is a member of the Second Baptist Church since its organization in 1892.

Having passed her three score and ten years she is "ready to go when the Lord calls her."

WPA in Ohio
Federal Writers' Project
Bishop & Isleman
Reporter: Bishop
(Revision)
July 8, 1937

Topic: Ex-Slaves
Jefferson County, District #5

JOHN WILLIAMS MATHEUS

"My mothers name was Martha. She died when I was eleven months old. My mother was owned by Racer Blue and his wife Scotty. When I was bout eleven or twelve they put me out with Michael Blue and his wife Mary. Michael Blue was a brother to Racer Blue. Racer Blue died when I was three or four. I have a faint rememberance of him dying suddenly one night and see him laying out. He was the first dead person I saw and it seemed funny to me to see him laying there so stiff and still."

"I remember the Yankee Soldier, a string of them on horses, coming through Springfield, W. Va. It was like a circus parade. What made me remember that, was a colored man standing near me who had a new hat on his head. A soldier came by and saw the hat and he took it off the colored man's head, and put his old dirty one on the colored man's head and put the nice new one on his own head."

"I think Abraham Lincoln the greatest man that ever lived. He belonged to no church; but he sure was Christian. I think he was born for the time and if he lived longer he would have done lots of good for the colored people."

"I wore jeans and they got so stiff when they were wet that they would stand up. I wore boots in the winter, but none in the summer."

"When slavery was going on there was the 'underground railway' in Ohio. But after the surrender some of the people in Ohio were not so good to the colored people. The old folks told me they were stoned when they came across the river to Ohio after the surrender and that the colored people were treated like cats and dogs."

"Mary Blue had two daughters, both a little older than me and I played with them. One day they went to pick berries. When they came back they left the berries on the table in the kitchen and went to the front room to talk to their mother. I remember the two steps down to the room and I came to listen to them tell about berry pickin'. Then their mother told me to go sweep the kitchen. I went and took the broom and saw the berries. I helped myself to the berries. Mary wore soft shoes, so I did not hear her coming until she was nearly in the room. I had berries in my hand and I closed my hand around the handle of the broom with the berries in my hand. She says, 'John, what are you doin'? I say, 'nothin'. Den she say, 'Let me see your hand! I showed her my hand with nothin' in it. She say, 'let me see the other hand! I had to show her my hand with the berries all crushed an the juice on my hand and on the handle of the broom."

"Den she say; 'You done two sins'. 'You stole the

berries!, I don't mind you having the berries, but you should have asked for them. 'You stole them and you have sinned. 'Den you told a lie! She says, 'John I must punish you, I want you to be a good man; don't try to be a great man, be a good man then you will be a great man! She got a switch off a peach tree and she gave me a good switching. I never forgot being caught with the berries and the way she talked bout my two sins. That hurt me worse than the switching. I never stole after that."

"I stayed with Michael and Mary Blue till I was nineteen. They were supposed to give me a saddle and bridle, clothes and a hundred dollars. The massa made me mad one day. I was rendering hog fat. When the crackling would fizzle, he hollo and say 'don't put so much fire.' He came out again and said, 'I told you not to put too much fire,' and he threatened to give me a thrashing. I said, 'If you do I will throw rocks at you.'"

"After that I decided to leave and I told Anna Blue I was going. She say, 'Don't do it, you are too young to go out into the world.' I say, I don't care, and I took a couple of sacks and put in a few things and walked to my uncle. He was a farmer at New Creek. He told me he would get me a job at his brothers farm until they were ready to use me in the tannary. He gave me eight dollars a month until the tanner got ready to use me. I went to the tanner and worked for eight dollars a week. Then I came to Steubenville. I got work and stayed in Steubenville 18 months. Then I went back and returned to Steubenville in 1884."

• Word Picture of JOHN WILLIAM MATHEUS

John William Matheus Mr. John William Matheus is about 5'4" and weighs about 130 pounds. He looks smart in his bank messenger uniform. On his sleeve he wears nine stripes. Each stripe means five years service. Two years were served before he earned his first strip, so that gives him a total of 47 years service for the Union Savings Bank and Trust Company, Steubenville, Ohio. He also wears a badge which designates him as a deputy sheriff of Jefferson County.

Mr. Matheus lives with his wife at 203 Dock Street. This moderate sized and comfortable home he has owned for over 40 years. His first wife died several years ago. During his first marriage nine children came to them. In his second marriage one child was born.

His oldest son is John Frederick Matheus. He is a professor at [Charleston] [HW: West Virginia] State College Institute. He was born in Steubenville and graduated from Steubenville High School. Later he studied in Cleveland and New York. He speaks six languages fluently and is the author of many published short stories.

Two other sons are employed in the post office, one is a mail carrier and the other is a janitor. His only daughter is a domestic servant.

Mr. Matheus attended school in Springfield, W. Va., for four years. When he came to Steubenville he attended night school for two winters. Mr. Dorhman J. Sinclair who founded the Union Savings Bank and Trust Co., employed Mr. Matheus from the beginning and in recognition of his loyal service bequeated to Mr. Matheus a pension of fifty dollars per month.

Mr. Matheus is a member of the office board of the

Quinn Memorial A.M.E. He has been an elder of that church for many years and also trustee and treasure. He frequently serves on the jury. He is well known and highly respected in the community.

United States. Work Projects Administration

WPA in Ohio
Federal Writers' Project
Bishop & Isleman
Reporter: Bishop
(Revision)
July 8, 1937

Topic: Ex-Slaves
Jefferson County, District #5

JOHN WILLIAMS MATHEUS

"My mothers name was Martha. She died when I was eleven months old. My mother was owned by Racer Blue and his wife Scotty. When I was bout eleven or twelve they put me out with Michael Blue and his wife Mary. Michael Blue was a brother to Racer Blue. Racer Blue died when I was three or four. I have a faint rememberance of him dying suddenly one night and see him laying out. He was the first dead person I saw and it seemed funny to me to see him laying there so stiff and still."

"I remember the Yankee Soldier, a string of them on horses, coming through Springfield, W. Va. It was like a circus parade. What made me remember that, was a colored man standing near me who had a new hat on his head. A soldier came by and saw the hat and he took it off the colored man's head, and put his old dirty one on the colored man's head and put the nice new one on his own head."

"I think Abraham Lincoln the greatest man that ever lived. He belonged to no church; but he sure was Christian. I think he was born for the time and if he lived longer he would have done lots of good for the colored people."

"I wore jeans and they got so stiff when they were wet that they would stand up. I wore boots in the winter, but none in the summer."

"When slavery was going on there was the 'underground railway' in Ohio. But after the surrender some of the people in Ohio were not so good to the colored people. The old folks told me they were stoned when they came across the river to Ohio after the surrender and that the colored people were treated like cats and dogs."

"Mary Blue had two daughters, both a little older than me and I played with them. One day they went to pick berries. When they came back they left the berries on the table in the kitchen and went to the front room to talk to their mother. I remember the two steps down to the room and I came to listen to them tell about berry pickin'. Then their mother told me to go sweep the kitchen. I went and took the broom and saw the berries. I helped myself to the berries. Mary wore soft shoes, so I did not hear her coming until she was nearly in the room. I had berries in my hand and I closed my hand around the handle of the broom with the berries in my hand. She says, 'John, what are you doin'? I say, 'nothin'. Den she say, 'Let me see your hand! I showed her my hand with nothin' in it. She say, 'let me see the other hand! I had to show her my hand with the berries all crushed an the juice on my hand and on the handle of the broom."

"Den she say; 'You done two sins'. 'You stole the

berries!, I don't mind you having the berries, but you should have asked for them. 'You stole them and you have sinned. 'Den you told a lie! She says, 'John I must punish you, I want you to be a good man; don't try to be a great man, be a good man then you will be a great man! She got a switch off a peach tree and she gave me a good switching. I never forgot being caught with the berries and the way she talked bout my two sins. That hurt me worse than the switching. I never stole after that."

"I stayed with Michael and Mary Blue till I was nineteen. They were supposed to give me a saddle and bridle, clothes and a hundred dollars. The massa made me mad one day. I was rendering hog fat. When the crackling would fizzle, he hollo and say 'don't put so much fire.' He came out again and said, 'I told you not to put too much fire,' and he threatened to give me a thrashing. I said, 'If you do I will throw rocks at you.'"

"After that I decided to leave and I told Anna Blue I was going. She say, 'Don't do it, you are too young to go out into the world.' I say, I don't care, and I took a couple of sacks and put in a few things and walked to my uncle. He was a farmer at New Creek. He told me he would get me a job at his brothers farm until they were ready to use me in the tannary. He gave me eight dollars a month until the tanner got ready to use me. I went to the tanner and worked for eight dollars a week. Then I came to Steubenville. I got work and stayed in Steubenville 18 months. Then I went back and returned to Steubenville in 1884."

United States. Work Projects Administration

• Word Picture of JOHN WILLIAM MATHEUS

Mr. John William Matheus is about 5'4" and weighs about 130 pounds. He looks smart in his bank messenger uniform. On his sleeve he wears nine stripes. Each stripe means five years service. Two years were served before he earned his first strip, so that gives him a total of 47 years service for the Union Savings Bank and Trust Company, Steubenville, Ohio. He also wears a badge which designates him as a deputy sheriff of Jefferson County.

Mr. Matheus lives with his wife at 203 Dock Street. This moderate sized and comfortable home he has owned for over 40 years. His first wife died several years ago. During his first marriage nine children came to them. In his second marriage one child was born.

His oldest son is John Frederick Matheus. He is a professor at [Charleston] [HW: West Virginia] State College Institute. He was born in Steubenville and graduated from Steubenville High School. Later he studied in Cleveland and New York. He speaks six languages fluently and is the author of many published short stories.

Two other sons are employed in the post office, one is a mail carrier and the other is a janitor. His only daughter is a domestic servant.

Mr. Matheus attended school in Springfield, W. Va., for four years. When he came to Steubenville he attended night school for two winters. Mr. Dorhman J. Sinclair who founded the Union Savings Bank and Trust Co., employed Mr. Matheus from the beginning and in recognition of his loyal service bequeated to Mr. Matheus a pension of fifty dollars per month.

Mr. Matheus is a member of the office board of the Quinn Memorial A.M.E. He has been an elder of that church for many years and also trustee and treasure. He frequently serves on the jury. He is well known and highly respected in the community.

United States. Work Projects Administration

Sarah Probst, Reporter
Audrey Meighen, Author-Editor

Folklore: Ex-Slaves
Meigs County, District Three

MR. WILLIAM NELSON
Aged 88

WILLIAM NELSON

"Whar's I bawned? 'Way down Belmont Missouri, jes' cross frum C'lumbus Kentucky on de Mississippi. Oh, I 'lows 'twuz about 1848, caise I wuz fo'teen when Marse Ben done brung me up to de North home with him in 1862."

"My Pappy, he wuz 'Kaintuck', John Nelson an' my mammy wuz Junis Nelson. No suh, I don't know whar dey wuz bawned, first I member 'bout wuz my pappy buildin' railroad in Belmont. Yes suh, I had five sistahs and bruthahs. Der names—lets see—Oh yes—der wuz, John, Jim, George, Suzan and Ida. No, I don't member nothin' 'bout my gran'parents."

"My mammy had her own cabin for hur and us chilluns. De wuz rails stuck through de cracks in de logs fo' beds with straw on top fo' to sleep on."

"What'd I do, down dar on plantashun? I hoed corn, tatahs, garden onions, and hepped take cair de hosses, mules an oxen. Say—I could hoe onions goin' backwards. Yessuh, I cud."

"De first money I see wuz what I got frum sum soljers fo' sellin' dem a bucket of turtl' eggs. Dat wuz de day I run away to see sum Yankee steamboats filled with soljers."

"Marse Dick, Marse Beckwith's son used to go fishin' with me. Wunce we ketched a fish so big it tuk three men to tote it home. Yes suh, we always had plenty to eat. What'd I like best? Corn pone, ham, bacon, chickens, ducks and possum. My mammy had hur own garden. In de summah men folks weah overalls, and de womins weah cotton and all of us went barefooted. In de winter we wore shoes made on de plantashun. I wuzn't married 'til aftah I come up North to Ohio."

"Der wuz Marse Beckwith, mighty mean ol' devel; Miss Lucy, his wife, and de chilluns, Miss Manda, Miss Nan, and Marse Dick, and the other son wuz killed in der war at Belmont. Deir hous' wuz big and had two stories and porticoes and den Marse Beckwith owned land with cabins on 'em whar de slaves lived."

"No suh, we didn't hab no driver, ol' Marse dun his own drivin'. He was a mean ol' debel and whipped his slaves of'n and hard. He'd make 'em strip to the waist then he's lash 'em with his long blacksnake whip. Ol' Marse he'd whip womin same as men. I member seein' 'im whip my mammy wunce. Marse Beckwith used the big smoke hous' for de jail. I neber see no slaves sold but I have seen 'em loaned and traded off."

"I member one time a slave named Tom and his wife, my mammy an' me tried to run away, but we's ketched and brung back. Ol' Marse whipped Tom and my mammy and den sent Tom off on a boat."

"One day a white man tol' us der wuz a war and sum day we'd be free."

"I neber heard of no 'ligion, baptizing', nor God, nor Heaven, de Bible nor education down on de plantashun, I gues' dey didn't hab nun of 'em. When Marse Ben brung me North to Ohio with him wuz first time I knowed 'bout such things. Marse Ben and Miss Lucy mighty good to me, sent me to school and tole me 'bout God and Heaven and took me to Church. No, de white folks down dar neber hepped me to read or write."

"The slaves wus always tiahed when dey got wurk dim in evenins' so dey usually went to bed early so dey'd be up fo' clock next mornin'. On Christmas Day dey always had big dinna but no tree or gifts."

"How'd I cum North? Well, one day I run 'way from plantashun and hunted 'til I filled a bucket full turtl' eggs den I takes dem ovah on river what I hears der's sum Yankee soljers and de soljers buyed my eggs and hepped me on board de boat. Den Marse Ben, he wuz Yankee ofser, tol 'em he take cair me and he did. Den Marse Ben got sick and cum home and brung me along and I staid with 'em 'til I wuz 'bout fo'ty, when I gets married and moved to Wyllis Hill. My wife, was Mary Williams, but she died long time 'go and so did our little son, since dat time I've lived alone."

"Yessuh, I'se read 'bout Booker Washington."

"I think Abraham Lincoln wuz a mighty fine man, he is de 'Saint of de colured race'."

"Good day suh."

United States. Work Projects Administration

WPA in Ohio
Federal Writers' Project
Bishop & Isleman
Jun 9, 1937

Topic: Ex-Slaves
Jefferson County, District #2

MRS. CATHERINE SLIM
Ex-slave, 87 years,
939 N. 6th St., Steubenville

CATHERINE SLIM

I wuz born in Rockingham, Virginny; a beautiful place where I cum from. My age is en de courthouse, Harrisonburg, Virginny. I dunno de date of my birth, our massa's wouldn't tell us our age.

My mother's name wuz Sally. She wuz a colored woman and she died when I wuz a little infant. I don't remember her. She had four chillun by my father who wuz a white man. His name wuz Jack Rose. He made caskets for de dead people.

My mother had six chillun altogether. De name of de four by my father wuz, Frances de oldest sister, Sarah wuz next, den Mary. I am de baby, all three are dead cept me. I am very last one livin'.

I had two half-brudders, dey were slaves too, John and Berwin. Berwin wuz drowned in W. Va. He wuz bound out to Hamsburger and drowned just after he got free. Dey did not sold infant slaves. Den dey bound out by de court. John got free and went to Liberia and died after he got there. He wuz my oldest brudder.

I wuz bound out by de court to Marse Barley and Miss Sally. I had to git up fore daylight and look at de clock wid de candle. I held up de candle to de clock, but couldn't tell de time. Den dey ask me if de little hand wuz on three mark or four mark. Dey wouldn't tell me de time but bye and bye I learned de time myself.

I asked de mistress to learn me a book and she sez, "Don't yo know we not allowed to learn you niggers nothin', don't ask me dat no more. I'll kill you if you do." I wuzn't goin' to ask her dat anymore.

When I wuz ten years old I wuz doin' women's work. I learned to do a little bit of eberthin'. I worked on de farm and I worked in de house. I learned to do a little bit of eberthin'. On de farm I did eberthin' cept plow.

I lived in a nice brick house. En de front wuz de valley pike. It wuz four and three-quarter miles to Harrisonburg and three and three-quarter miles to Mt. Crawford. It wuz a lobley place and a fine farm.

I used to sleep in a waggoner's bed. It wuz like a big bed-comfort, stuffed with wool. I laid it on de floor and sleep on it wid a blanket ober me, when I get up I roll up de bed and push it under de mistress's bed.

I earned money, but nebber got it. Dey wuz so mean I run away. I think dey wuz so mean dat dey make me run away and den dey wouldn't heb to pay de money. If I could roll up my sleeve I could show you a mark that cum from a beatin' I had wid a cow-hide whip. Dey whip me for nothin'.

After I run away I had around until the surrender cum. Eberybody cum to life then. It wuz a hot time in de ole place when dey sezs freedom. The colored ones jumped straight up and down.

De feed us plenty. We had pork, corn, rabbit, dey hed eberythin' nice. Dey made us stan' up to eat. Dey no low us sit down to eat. Der wuz bout twenty or thirty slaves on de farm an some ob dem hed der own gardens. Anythin' dey gib us to eat I liked. Dey had bees and honey.

I wore little calico dress in de summer, white, red, and blue. Some hed flowers and some hed strips. We went barefooted until Christmas. Den dey gabe us shoes. De shoes were regular ole common shoes; not eben calfskin. Dey weaved linen and made us our clothes. Dey hab sleeves, plain body and little skirt. I hed two of dem for winter.

I hab seen lots of slaves chained together, goin' south, some wuz singin' and some wuz cryin'. Some hed dey chillun and some didn't.

Dey took me to church wid dem and dey put me behind de door. Dey tole me to set der till dey cum out. And when I see dem cumin' out to follow behind and get into de carrage. I dursent say nothin'. I wuz like a petty dog.

United States. Work Projects Administration

Slave Narratives

INTERVIEW OF EX-SLAVE FROM VIRGINIA
Reported by Rev. Edward Knox
Jun. 9, 1937

Topic: Ex-slaves
Guernsey County, District #2

JENNIE SMALL
Ex-slave, over 80 years of age

JENNIE SMALL

I was born in Pocahontas County, Virginia in the drab and awful surroundings of slavery. The whipping post and cruelty in general made an indelible impression in my mind. I can see my older brothers in their tow-shirts that fell knee-length which was sometimes their only garment, toiling laborously under a cruel lash as the burning sun beamed down upon their backs.

Pappy McNeal (we called the master Pappy) was cruel and mean. Nothing was too hard, too sharp, or too heavy to throw at an unfortunate slave. I was very much afraid of him; I think as much for my brothers' sakes as for my own. Sometimes in his fits of anger, I was afraid he might kill someone. However, one happy spot in my heart was for his son-in-law who told us: "Do not call Mr. McNeal the master, no one is your master but God, call Mr. McNeal, mister." I have always had a tender spot in my heart for him.

There are all types of farm work to do and also some repair work about the barns and carriages. It was one of these carriages my brother was repairing when the Yankees came, but I am getting ahead of my story.

I was a favorite of my master. I had a much better sleeping quarters than my brothers. Their cots were made of straw or corn husks. Money was very rare but we were all well-fed and kept. We wore tow-shirts which were knee-length, and no shoes. Of course, some of the master's favorites had some kind of footwear.

There were many slaves on our plantation. I never saw any of them auctioned off or put in chains. Our master's way of punishment was the use of the whipping post. When we received cuts from the whip he put soft soap and salt into our wounds to prevent scars. He did not teach us any reading or writing; we had no special way of learning; we picked up what little we knew.

When we were ill on our plantation, Dr. Wallace, a relative of Master McNeal, took care of us. We were always taught to fear the Yankees. One day I was playing in the yard of our master, with the master's little boy. Some Yankee Soldiers came up and we hid, of course, because we had been taught to fear the soldiers. One Yankee soldier discovered me, however, and took me on his knee and told me that they were our friends end not our enemies; they were here to help us. After that I loved them instead of fearing them. When we received our freedom, our master was very sorry, because we had always done all their work, and hard labor.

Geo. H. Conn, Writer
Wilbur C. Ammon, Editor
C.R. McLean, District Supervisor
June 11, 1937

Folklore
Summit County, District #5

ANNA SMITH

In a little old rocking chair, sits an old colored "mammy" known to her friends as "Grandma" Smith, spending the remaining days with her grandchildren. Small of stature, tipping the scales at about 100 lbs. but alert to the wishes and cares of her children, this old lady keeps posted on current events from those around her. With no stoop or bent back and with a firm step she helps with the housework and preparing of meals, waiting, when permitted, on others. In odd moments, she like to work at her favorite task of "hooking" rag rugs. Never having worn glasses, her eyesight is the envy of the younger generation. She spends most of the time at home, preferring her rocker and pipe (she has been smoking for more than eighty year) to a back seat in an automobile.

When referring to Civil War days, her eyes flash and words flow from her with a fluency equal to that of any youngster. Much of her speech is hard to understand as she reverts to the early idiom and pronunciation of her race. Her head, tongue, arms and hands all move at the same time as she talks.

A note of hesitancy about speaking of her past shows

at times when she realizes she is talking to one not of her own race, but after eight years in the north, where she has been treated courteously by her white neighbors, that old feeling of inferiority under which she lived during slave days and later on a plantation in Kentucky has about disappeared.

Her home is comfortably furnished two story house with a front porch where, in the comfort of an old rocking chair, she smokes her pipe and dreams as the days slip away. Her children and their children are devoted to her. With but a few wants or requests her days a re quiet and peaceful.

Kentucky with its past history still retains its hold. She refers to it as "God's Chosen Land" and would prefer to end her days where about eighty years of her life was spent.

On her 101st birthday (1935) she posed for a picture, seated in her favorite chair with her closest friend, her pipe.

Abraham Lincoln is as big a man with her today as when he freed her people.

With the memories of the Civil War still fresh in her mind and and secret longing to return to her Old Kentucky Home, Mrs. Anna Smith, born in May of 1833 and better known to her friends as "Grandma" Smith, is spending her remaining days with her grandchildren, in a pleasant home at 518 Bishop Street.

On a plantation owned by Judge Toll, on the banks of the Ohio River at Henderson, Ke., Anna (Toll) Smith was born. From her own story, and information gathered from other sources the year 1835 is as near a correct date as possible to obtain.

Anna Smith's parents were William Clarke and Miranda Toll. Her father was a slave belonging to Judge Toll. It was common practice for slaves to assume the last name of their owners.

It was before war was declared between the north and south that she was married, for she claims her daughter was "going on three" when President Lincoln freed the slaves. Mrs. Smith remembers her father who died at the age of 117 years.

Her oldest brother was 50 when he joined the confederate army. Three other brothers were sent to the front. One was an ambulance attendant, one belonged to the cavalry, one an orderly seargeant and the other joined the infantry. All were killed in action. Anna Smith's husband later joined the war and was reported killed.

When she became old enough for service she was taken into the "Big House" of her master, where she served as kitchen helper, cook and later as nurse, taking care of her mistress' second child.

She learned her A.B.C.'s by listening to the tutor teaching the children of Judge Toll.

"Grandma" Smith's vision is the wonder of her friends. She has never worn glasses and can distinguish objects and people at a distance as readily as at close range. She occupies her time by hooking rag rugs and doing housework and cooking. She is "on the go" most of the time, but when need for rest overtakes her, she resorts to her easy chair, a pipeful of tobacco and a short nap and she is ready to carry on.

Many instances during those terrible war days are fresh in her mind: men and boys, in pairs and groups passing the "big house" on their way to the recruiting station on the public square, later going back in squads and companies to fight; Yankee soldiers raiding the plantation, taking corn and hay or whatever could be used by the northern army; and continual apprehension for the menfolk at the front.

She remembers the baying of blood hounds at night along the Ohio River, trying to follow the scent of escaping negroes and the crack of firearms as white people, employed by the plantation owners attempted to halt the negroes in their efforts to cross the Ohio River into Ohio or to join the Federal army.

Referring to her early life, she recalls no special outstanding events. Her treatment from her master and mistress was pleasant, always receiving plenty of food and clothing but never any money.

In a grove not far from the plantation home, the slaves from the nearby estates meet on Sunday for worship. Here under the spreading branches they gathered for religious worship and to exchange news.

When President Lincoln issued his proclamation freeing the slaves, and the news reached the plantation, she went to her master to learn if she was free. On learning it was true she returned to her parents who were living on another plantation.

She has been living with her grandchildren for the

past nine years, contented but ready to go when the "Good Lord calls her."

United States. Work Projects Administration

Sarah Probst, Reporter
Audrey Meighen, Author-Editor
Jun 9, 1937

Folklore
Meigs County, District Three
[HW: Middeport]

NAN STEWART

"I'se bawned Charl'stun, West Virginia in February 1850."

"My mammy's name? Hur name wuz Kath'run Paine an' she wuz bawned down Jackson County, Virginia. My pappy wuz John James, a coopah an' he wuz bawned at Rock Creek, West Virginia. He cum'd ovah heah with Lightburn's Retreat. Dey all crossed de ribah at Buffington Island. Yes, I had two bruthahs and three sistahs. Deir wuz Jim, Thomas, he refugeed from Charl'stun to Pum'roy and it tuk him fo' months, den de wuz sistah Adah, Carrie an' Ella. When I rite young I wurked as hous' maid fo' numbah quality white folks an' latah on I wuz nurs' fo' de chilluns in sum homes, heah abouts."

"Oh, de slaves quartahs, dey wuz undah de sam' ruf with Marse Hunt's big hous' but in de back. When I'se littl' I sleeped in a trun'l bed. My mammy wuz mighty 'ticlar an' clean, why she made us chilluns wash ouah feets ebry night fo' we git into de bed."

"When Marse Hunt muved up to Charl'stun, my mammy and pappy liv' in log cabin."

"My gran' mammy, duz I 'member hur? Honey chile, I shure duz. She wuz my pappy's mammy. She wuz one hun'erd and fo' yeahs ol' when she die rite in hur cheer. Dat mawhin' she eat a big hearty brekfast. One day I 'member she sezs to Marse Hunt, 'I hopes you buys hun'erds an' hun'erds ob slaves an' neber sells a one. Hur name wuz Erslie Kizar Chartarn."

"Marse an' missus, mighty kind to us slaves. I lurned to sew, piece quilts, clean de brass an' irons an' dog irons. Most time I set with de ol' ladies, an' light deir pipes, an' tote 'em watah, in gourds. I us' tu gether de turkey eggs an' guinea eggs an' sell 'em. I gits ten cents duzen fo' de eggs. Marse and Missus wuz English an' de count money like dis—fo' pence, ha' penny. Whut I do with my money? Chile I saved it to buy myself a nankeen dress."

"Yes mam we always had plenty to eat. What'd I like bes' to eat, waffl's, honey and stuffed sausage, but I spise possum and coon. Marse Hunt had great big meat hous' chuck full all kinds of meats. Say, do you all know Marse used to keep stuffed sausage in his smoke hous' fo' yeahs an' it wuz shure powahful good when it wuz cooked. Ouah kitchin wuz big an' had great big fiah place whur we'd bake ouah bread in de ashes. We baked ouah corn pone an' biskets in a big spidah. I still have dat spidah an' uses it."

"By the way you knows Squire Gellison wuz sum fishahman an' shure to goodness ketched lots ob fish. Why he'd ketch so many, he'd clean 'em, cut 'em up, put 'em in half barrels an' pass 'em 'round to de people on de farms."

"Most de slaves on Marse Hunt's place had dir own

garden patches. Sumtimes dey'd have to hoe the gardens by moonlight. Dey sell deir vegetables to Marse Hunt."

"In de summah de women weah dresses and apruns made ob linen an' men weah pants and shurts ob linen. Linsey-woolsey and jean wuz woven on de place fo' wintah clothes. We had better clothes to weah on Sunday and we weahed shoes on Sunday. The' shoes and hoots wuz made on de plantashun."

"My mastah wuz Marse Harley Hunt an' his wife wuz Miss Maria Sanders Hunt. Marse and Miss Hunt didn't hab no chilluns of der own but a nephew Marse Oscar Martin and niece Miss Mary Hunt frum Missouri lived with 'em. Dey's all kind to us slaves. De Hous' wuz great big white frame with picket fence all 'round de lot. When we lived Charl'stun Marse Hunt wuz a magistrate. Miss Hunt's muthah and two aunts lived with 'em."

"No mam, we didn't hab no ovahseeah. Marse Hunt had no use fo' ovahseeahs, fact is he 'spise 'em. De oldah men guided de young ones in deir labors. The poor white neighbahs wurn't 'lowed to live very close to de plantashun as Marse Hunt wanted de culured slave chilluns to be raised in propah mannah."

"I duzn't know how many acres in de plantashun. Deir wuz only 'bout three or fo' cabins on de place. Wurk started 'bout seben clock 'cept harvest time when ebrybudy wuz up early. De slaves didn't wurk so hard nor bery late at night. Slaves wuz punished by sendin' 'em off to bed early.

"When I'se livin' at Red House I seed slaves auctioned off. Ol' Marse Veneable sold ten or lebin slaves, women and chilluns, to niggah tradahs way down farthah south. I well 'members day Aunt Millie an' Uncl' Edmund wuz sold—dir son Harrison wuz bought by Marse Hunt. 'Twuz shure sad an' folks cried when Aunt Millie and Uncl' Edmund wuz tuk away. Harrison neber see his mammy an' pappy agin. Slaves wuz hired out by de yeah fo' nine hundred dollahs."

"Marse Hunt had schools fo' de slaves chilluns. I went to school on Lincoln Hill, too."

"Culured preachahs use to cum to plantashun an' dey would read de Bible to us. I 'member one special passage preachahs read an' I neber understood it 'til I cross de riber at Buffinton Island. It wuz, 'But they shall sit every man under his own vine and under his fig tree; and none shall make them afraid; for the mouth of the Lord of Hosts hath spoken it." Micah 4:4. Den I knows it is de fulfillment ob dat promis; 'I would soon be undah my own vine an' fig tree' and hab no feah of bein' sold down de riber to a mean Marse. I recalls der wuz Thorton Powell, Ben Sales and Charley Releford among de preachahs. De church wuz quite aways frum de hous'. When der'd be baptizins de sistahs and brethruns would sing 'Freely, freely will you go with me, down to the riber'. 'Freely, freely quench your thirst Zion's sons and daughtahs'."

"How wells I 'member when I wuz converted. I'd thought 'bout 'ligion a lot but neber wunce wuz I muved to repent. One day I went out to cut sum wood an' begin thinkin' agin and all wunce I feeled so relieved an' good an' run home to tell granny an' de uthahs dat I'd cum out at last."

"No, we didn't wurk on Saturday aftahnoons.

Christmas wuz big time at Marse Hunts hous'. Preparations wuz made fo' it two weeks fo' day cum. Der wuz corn sings an' big dances, 'ceptin' at 'ligious homes. Der wuz no weddins' at Marse Hunts, cause dey had no chilluns an' de niece and nephew went back to own homes to git married."

"We played sich games as marbles; yarn ball; hop, skip, an' jump; mumble peg an' pee wee. Wunce I's asked to speak down to white chilluns school an' dis is what I speak:

> 'The cherries are ripe,
> The cherries are ripe,
> Oh give the baby one,
> The baby is too little to chew,
> The robin I see up in the tree,
> Eating his fill and shaking his bill,
> And down his throat they run.'

Another one:

> 'Tobacco is an Indian weed,
> And from the devil doth proceed
> It robs the pocket and burns the clothes
> And makes a chimney of the nose.'

"When de slaves gits sick, deir mammies luked af'er em but de Marse gived de rem'dies. Yes, dere wuz dif'runt kinds, salts, pills, Castah orl, herb teas, garlic, 'fedia, sulphah, whiskey, dog wood bark, sahsaparilla an' apple root. Sometimes charms wuz used.

"I 'member very well de day de Yankees cum. De slaves

all cum a runnin' an' yellin': "Yankees is cumin', Yankee soljers is comin', hurrah". Bout two or three clock, we herd bugles blowing' an' guns on Taylah Ridge. Kids wuz playin' an' all 'cited. Sumone sed: "Kathrun, sumthin' awful gwine happen", an' sumone else sez; "De' is de Yankees". De Yankee mens camp on ouah farm an' buyed ouah buttah, milk an' eggs. Marse Hunt, whut you all call 'bilionist [HW: abolitionist] an' he wuz skeered of suthern soljers an' went out to de woods an' laid behind a log fo' seben weeks and seben days, den he 'cided to go back home. He sez he had a dream an' prayed, "I had bettah agone, but I prayed. No use let des debils take you, let God take you." We tote food an' papahs to Marse while he wuz a hidin'."

"One ob my prized possessions is Abraham Lincoln's pictures an' I'se gwine to gib it to a culured young man whose done bin so kind to me, when I'se gone. Dat's Bookah T. Washington's picture ovah thar."

"I'se married heah in Middeport by Preachah Bill, 1873. My husban' wuz Charles Stewart, son of Johnny Stewart. Deir wuz hous' full my own folks, mammy, pappy, sistahs, bruthas, an' sum white folks who cumed in to hep dress me up fo' de weddin'. We kep de weddin' a secrut an' my aunt butted hur horns right off tryin' to fin' out when it wuz. My husban' had to leave right away to go to his job on de boat. We had great big dinnah, two big cakes an' ice cream fo' desurt. We had fo'teen chilluns with only two livin'. I has five gran' sons an' two great gran' daughters."

"Goodbye—cum back agin."

Slave Narratives

Miriam Logan, Lebanon, Ohio
Warren County, Dist. 2
July 2, 1937

Interview with SAMUEL SUTTON, Ex Slave.
Born in Garrett County, Kentucky, in 1854.

SAMUEL SUTTON

(drawing of Sutton) [TR: no drawing found]

"Yes'em, I sho were bo'n into slavery. Mah mothah were a cook—(they was none betteah)—an she were sold four times to my knownin'. She were part white, for her fathah were a white man. She live to be seventy-nine yeahs an nine months old."

"Ah was bo'n in Garrett County, but were raised by ol' Marster Ballinger in Knox County, an' ah don remember nothin 'bout Garrett County." When Lincoln was elected last time, I were about eight yeahs ol'."

"Ol' Marster own 'bout 400-acres, n' ah don' know how many slaves—maybe 30. He'd get hard up fo money n' sell one or two; then he'd get a lotta work on hands, an maybe buy one or two cheap,—go 'long lak dat you see." He were a good man, Ol' Mars Ballinger were—a preacher, an he wuk hisse'f too. Ol' Mis' she pretty cross sometime, but ol' Mars, he weren't no mean man, an ah don' 'member he evah whip us. Yes'em dat ol' hous is still standin' on the Lexington-Lancaster Pike, and las time I know, Baby Marster he were still livin."

"Ol' Mars. tuk us boys out to learn to wuk when we was

both right little me and Baby Mars. Ah wuz to he'p him, an do what he tol' me to—an first thing ah members is a learnin to hoe de clods. Corn an wheat Ol' Mars. raised, an he sets us boys out fo to learn to wuk. Soon as he lef' us Baby Mars, he'd want to eat; send me ovah to de grocery fo sardines an' oysters. Nevah see no body lak oyster lak he do! Ah do n' lak dem. Ol Mars. scold him—say he not only lazy hese'f, but he make me lazy too."

"De Wah? Yes'em ah sees soldiers, Union Calvary [HW: Cavalry] goin' by, dressed fine, wid gold braid on blue, an big boots. But de Rebels now, I recollect dey had no uniforms fo dey wuz hard up, an dey cum in jes common clothes. Ol' Mars., he were a Rebel, an he always he'p 'em. Yes'em a pitched battle start right on our place. Didn't las' long, fo dey wuz a runnin fight on to Perryville, whaah de one big battle to take place in de State o' Kentucky, tuk place."

"Most likely story I remembers to tell you 'bout were somepin made me mad an I allus remember fo' dat. Ah had de bigges' fines' watermellon an ah wuz told to set up on de fence wid de watermellon an show 'em, and sell 'em fo twenty cents. Along cum a line o' soldiers."

"Heigh there boy!... How much for the mellon?" holler one at me.

"Twenty cents sir!" Ah say jes lak ah ben tol' to say; and he take dat mellon right out o' mah arms an' ride off widout payin' me. Ah run after dem, a tryin' to get mah money, but ah couldn't keep up wid dem soldiers on hosses; an all de soldiers jes' laf at me."

"Yes'em dat wuz de fines' big mellon ah evah see. Dat

wuz right mean in him—fine lookin gemman he were, at the head o' de line."

"Ol' Marster Ballinger, he were a Rebel, an he harbors Rebels. Dey wuz two men a hangin' around dere name o' Buell and Bragg."

"Buell were a nawtherner; Bragg, he were a Reb."

"Buell give Bragg a chance to get away, when he should have found out what de Rebs were doin' an a tuk him prisoner ah heard tell about dat."

"Dey wuz a lotta spyin', ridin' around dere fo' one thing and another, but ah don' know what it were all about. I does know ah feels sorry fo dem Rebel soldiers ah seen dat wuz ragged an tired, an all woe out, an Mars. He fell pretty bad about everything sometimes, but ah reckon dey wuz mean Rebs an southerners at had it all cumin' to em; ah allus heard tell dey had it comin' to em."

"Some ways I recollect times wuz lots harder after de War, some ways dey was better. But now a culled man ain't so much better off 'bout votin' an such some places yet, ah hears dat."

"Yes'em, they come an want hosses once in awhile, an they was a rarin' tarin' time atryin to catch them hosses fo they would run into the woods befo' you could get ahold of 'em. Morgan's men come fo hosses once, an ol Mars, get him's hosses, fo he were a Reb. Yes'em, but ah thinks them hosses got away from the Rebels; seem lak ah heard they did."

"Hosses? Ah wishes ah had me a team right now, and ah'd make me my own good livin! No'em, don't want no mule. They is set on havin they own way, an the contrariest critters! But a mule is a wuk animal, an eats little. Lotsa wuk in a mule. Mah boy, he say, 'quit wukin, an give us younguns a chance,' Sho nuf, they ain't the wuk they use to be, an the younguns needs it. Ah got me a pension, an a fine garden; ain't it fine now?"

"Yes'em, lak ah tells you, the wah were ovah, and the culled folks had a Big Time wid speakin'n everything ovah at Dick Robinsen's camp on de 4th. Nevah see such rejoicin on de Fourth 'o July since,-no'em, ah ain't."

"Ah seen two presidents, Grant an Hayes. I voted fo Hayes wen I wuz twenty-two yeahs old. General Grant, he were runnin against Greeley when ah heard him speak at Louieville. He tol what all Lincoln had done fo de culled man. Yes'em, fine lookin man he were, an he wore a fine suit. Yes'em ah ain't miss an election since ah were twenty-two an vote fo Hayes. Ah ain't gonto miss none, an ah vote lak the white man read outa de Emanicaption Proclamation, ah votes fo one ob Abe Lincoln's men ev'y time—ah sho do."

"Run a way slaves? No'em nevah know ed of any. Mars. Ballinger neighbor, old Mars. Tye—he harbor culled folks dat cum ask fo sumpin to eat in winter—n' he get 'em to stay awhile and do a little wuk fo him. Now, he did always have one or two 'roun dere dat way,—dat ah recollects—dat he didn't own. Maybe dey was runaway, maybe dey wuz just tramps an didn't belong to noboddy. Nevah hear o' anybody claimin' dem—dey stay awhile an wuk, den move on—den mo' cum, wuk while then move on. Mars. Tye—he get his wuk done dat way, cheap.

"No'em, don't believe in anything lak dat much. We

use to sprinkle salt in a thin line 'roun Mars. Ballinger's house, clear 'roun, to ward off quarellin an arguein' an ol' Miss Ballinger gettin a cross spell,—dat ah members, an then too;—ah don believe in payin out money on a Monday. You is liable to be a spendin an a losin' all week if you do. Den ah don' want see de new moon (nor ol' moon either) through, de branches o' trees. Ah know' a man dat see de moon tru de tree branches, an he were lookin' tru de bars 'a jail fo de month were out—an fo sumpin he nevah done either,—jus enuf bad luck—seein a moon through bush."

"Ah been married twice, an had three chillens. Mah oles' are Madge Hannah, an she sixty yeah ol' an still a teachin' at the Indian School where she been fo twenty-two yeahs now. She were trained at Berea in High School then Knoxville; then she get mo' learnin in Nashville in some course."

"Mah wife died way back yonder in 1884. Then when ah gets married again, mah wife am 32 when ah am 63. No'am, no mo' chillens. Ah lives heah an farms, an takes care ob mah sick girl, an mah boy, he live across the lane thah."

"No'em, no church, no meetin hous fo us culled people in Kentucky befo' de wah. Dey wuz prayin folks, and gets to meetin' at each othah's houses when dey is sumpin a pushin' fo prayer. No'em no school dem days, fo us." "Ol Mars., he were a preacher, he knowed de Bible, an tells out verses fo us—dats all ah members. Yes'em Ah am Baptist now, and ah sho do believe in a havin church."

"Ah has wuked on steam boats, an done railroad labor, an done a lotta farmin, an ah likes to farm best. Like to live in Ohio best. Ah can vote. If ah gits into trouble, de law give us a chance fo our property, same as if we were white. An we can vote lak white, widout no shootin, no fightin' about it—dats what ah likes. Nevah know white men to be so mean about anythin as dey is about votin some places—No'em, ah don't! Ah come heah in 1912. Ah was goin on to see mah daughter Madge Hannah in Oklahoma, den dis girl come to me paralized, an ah got me work heah in Lebanon, tendin cows an such at de creamery, an heah ah is evah since. Yes'em an ah don' wanto go no wheres else."

"No'em, no huntin' no mo. Useto hunt rabbit until las yeah. They ain't wuth the price ob a license no mo." No'em, ah ain't evah fished in Ohio."

"No'em, nevah wuz no singer, no time. Not on steamboats, nor nowheres. Don't member any songs, except maybe the holler we useto set up when dey wuz late wid de dinner when we wuked on de steamboat;— Dey sing-song lak dis:"

> 'Ol hen, she flew
> Ovah de ga-rden gate,
> Fo' she wuz dat hungrey
> She jes' couldn't wait.'

—but den dat ain't no real song."

"Kentucky river is place to fish—big cat fish. Cat fish an greens is good eatin. Ah seen a cat fish cum outa de Kentucky river 'lon as a man is tall; an them ol' fins slap mah laig when ah carries him ovah mah shoulder, an he tail draggin' on mah feet.—Sho nuf!"

"No'em, ah jes cain't tell you all no cryin sad story 'bout beatin' an a slave drivin, an ah don' know no ghost stories, ner nuthin'—ah is jes dumb dat way—ah's sorry 'bout it, but ah Jes—is."

Samuel Sutton lives in north lane Lebanon, just back of the French Creamery. He has one acre of land, a little unpainted, poorly furnished and poorly kept. His daughter is a huge fleshy colored woman wears a turban on her head. She has a fixed smile; says not a word. Samuel talks easily; answers questions directly; is quick in his movements. He is stooped and may 5'7" or 8" if standing straight. He wears an old fashioned "Walrus" mustache, and has a grey wooley fringe of hair about his smooth chocolate colored bald head. He is very dark in color, but his son is darker yet. His hearing is good. His sight very poor. Being so young when the Civil War was over, he remembers little or nothing about what the colored people thought or expected from freedom. He just remembers what a big time there was on that first "Free Fourth of July."

United States. Work Projects Administration

Ruth Thompson, Interviewing
Graff, Editing

Ex-Slave Interviews
Hamilton Co., District 12
Cincinnati

RICHARD TOLER
515 Poplar St.,
Cincinnati, O.

RICHARD TOLER

"Ah never fit in de wah; no suh, ah couldn't. Mah belly's been broke! But ah sho' did want to, and ah went up to be examined, but they didn't receive me on account of mah broken stomach. But ah sho' tried, 'cause ah wanted to be free. Ah didn't like to be no slave. Dat wasn't good times."

Richard Toler, 515 Poplar Street, century old former slave lifted a bony knee with one gnarled hand and crossed his legs, then smoothed his thick white beard. His rocking chair creaked, the flies droned, and through the open, unscreened door came the bawling of a calf from the building of a hide company across the street. A maltese kitten sauntered into the front room, which served as parlor and bedroom, and climbed complacently into his lap. In one corner a wooden bed was piled high with feather ticks, and bedecked with a crazy quilt and an number of small, brightly-colored pillows; a bureau opposite was laden to the edges with a collection of odds and ends—a one-legged alarm clock, a coal oil lamp, faded aritifical flowers in a gaudy vase, a pile of newspapers. A trunk against the wall was littered with several large books (one of which was the family Bible), a stack of dusty lamp shades, a dingy sweater, and several bushel-basket lids. Several packing cases and crates, a lard can full of cracked ice, a small, round oil heating stove, and an assorted lot of chairs completed the furnishings. The one decorative spot in the room was on the wall over the bed, where hung a large framed picture of Christ in The Temple. The two rooms beyond exhibited various broken-down additions to the heterogeneous collection.

"Ah never had no good times till ah was free", the old man continued. "Ah was bo'n on Mastah Tolah's (Henry Toler) plantation down in ole V'ginia, near Lynchburg in Campbell County. Mah pappy was a slave befo' me, and mah mammy, too. His name was Gawge Washin'ton Tolah, and her'n was Lucy Tolah. We took ouah name from ouah ownah, and we lived in a cabin way back of the big house, me and mah pappy and mammy and two brothahs.

"They nevah mistreated me, neithah. They's a whipping the slaves all the time, but ah run away all the time. And ah jus' tell them—if they whipped me, ah'd kill 'em, and ah nevah did get a whippin'. If ah thought one was comin' to me, Ah'd hide in the woods; then they'd send aftah me, and they say, 'Come, on back—we won't whip you'. But they killed some of the niggahs, whipped 'em to death. Ah guess they killed three or fo' on Tolah's place while ah was there.

"Ah nevah went to school. Learned to read and write mah name after ah was free in night school, but they nevah allowed us to have a book in ouah hand, and we couldn't have no money neither. If we had money we had to tu'n it ovah to ouah ownah. Chu'ch was not allowed in ouah pa't neithah. Ah go to the Meth'dist Chu'ch now, everybody ought to go. I think RELIGION MUST BE FINE, 'CAUSE GOD ALMIGHTY'S AT THE HEAD OF IT."

Toler took a small piece of ice from the lard can, popped it between his toothless gum, smacking enjoyment, swished at the swarming flies with a soiled rag handkerchief, and continued.

"Ah nevah could unnerstand about ghos'es. Nevah did see one. Lots of folks tell about seein' ghos'es, but ah nevah feared 'em. Ah was nevah raised up undah such supastitious believin's.

"We was nevah allowed no pa'ties, and when they had goin' ons at the big house, we had to clear out. Ah had to wo'k hard all the time every day in the week. Had to min' the cows and calves, and when ah got older ah had to hoe in the field. Mastah Tolah had about 500 acres, so they tell me, and he had a lot of cows and ho'ses and oxens, and he was a big fa'mer. Ah've done about evahthing in mah life, blacksmith and stone mason, ca'penter, evahthing but brick-layin'. Ah was a blacksmith heah fo' 36 yea's. Learned it down at Tolah's.

"Ah stayed on the plantation during the wah, and jes' did what they tol' me. Ah was 21 then. And ah walked 50 mile to vote for Gen'l Grant at Vaughn's precinct. Ah voted fo' him in two sessions, he run twice. And ah was 21 the fust time, cause they come and got me, and say, 'Come on now. You can vote now, you is 21.' And theah now—mah age is right theah. 'Bout as close as you can get it.

"Ah was close to the battle front, and I seen all dem famous men. Seen Gen'l Lee, and Grant, and Abe Lincoln. Seen John Brown, and seen the seven men that was hung with him, but we wasn't allowed to talk to any of 'em, jes' looked on in the crowd. Jes' spoke, and say 'How d' do.'

[HW: Harper's Ferry is not [TR: rest illegible]]

"But ah did talk to Lincoln, and ah tol' him ah wanted to be free, and he was a fine man, 'cause he made us all free. And ah got a ole histry, it's the Sanford American History, and was published in 1784[HW:18?]. But ah don't know where it is now, ah misplaced it. It is printed in the book, something ah said, not written by hand. And it says, 'Ah am a ole slave which has suvved fo' 21 yeahs, and ah would be quite pleased if you could help us to be free. We thank you very much. Ah trust that some day ah can do you the same privilege that you are doing for me. Ah have been a slave for many years.' (Note discrepancy).

"Aftah the wah, ah came to Cincinnati, and ah was married three times. Mah fust wife was Nannie. Then there was Mollie. They both died, and than ah was married Cora heah, and ah had six child'en, one girl and fo' boys. (Note discrepancy) They's two living yet; James is 70 and he is not married. And Bob's about thutty or fo'ty. Ah done lost al mah rememb'ance, too ole now. But Mollie died when he was bo'n, and he is crazy. He is out of Longview (Home for Mentally Infirm) now fo' a while, and he jes' wanders around, and wo'ks a little. He's not [TR: "not" is crossed out] ha'mless, he wouldn't hurt nobody. He ain't married neithah.

"After the wah, ah bought a fiddle, and ah was a good fiddlah. Used to be a fiddlah fo' the white girls to dance. Jes' picked it up, it was a natural gif'. Ah could still play if ah had a fiddle. Ah used to play at our hoe downs, too. Played all those ole time songs—Soldier's Joy, Jimmy Long Josey, Arkansas Traveler, and Black Eye Susie. Ah remembah the wo'ds to that one."

Smiling inwardly with pleasure as he again lived the past, the old Negro swayed and recited:

> Black Eye Susie, you look so fine,
> Black Eye Susie, ah think youah mine.
> A wondahful time we're having now,
> Oh, Black Eye Susie, ah believe that youah mine.

And away down we stomp aroun' the bush,
We'd think that we'd get back to wheah we could push
Black Eye Susie, ah think youah fine,
Black Eye Susie, Ah know youah mine.

Then, he resumed his conversational tone:

"Befo' the wah we nevah had no good times. They took good care of us, though. As pa'taculah with slaves as with the stock—that was their money, you know. And if we claimed a bein' sick, they'd give us a dose of castah oil and tu'pentine. That was the principal medicine cullud folks had to take, and sometimes salts. But nevah no whiskey—that was not allowed. And if we was real sick, they had the Doctah fo' us.

"We had very bad eatin'. Bread, meat, water. And they fed it to us in a trough, jes' like the hogs. And ah went in may shirt tail till I was 16, nevah had no clothes. And the flo' in ouah cabin was dirt, and at night we'd jes' take a blanket and lay down on the flo'. The dog was supe'ior to us; they would take him in the house.

"Some of the people I belonged to was in the Klu Klux Klan. Tolah had fo' girls and fo' boys. Some of those boys belonged. And I used to see them turn out. They went aroun' whippin' niggahs. They'd get young girls and strip 'em sta'k naked, and put 'em across barrels, and whip 'em till the blood run out of 'em, and then they would put salt in the raw pahts. And ah seen it, and it was as bloody aroun' em as if they'd stuck hogs.

"I sho' is glad I ain't no slave no moah. Ah thank God that ah lived to pas the yeahs until the day of 1937. Ah'm happy and satisfied now, and ah hopes ah see a million yeahs to come."

United States. Work Projects Administration

Forest H. Lees
C.R. McLean, Supervisor
June 10, 1937

Topic: Folkways
Medina County, District #5

JULIA WILLIAMS

Julia Williams, born in Winepark, Chesterfield County near Richmond, Virginia. Her age is estimated close to 100 years. A little more or a little less, it is not known for sure.

Her memory is becoming faded. She could remember her mothers name was Katharine but her father died when she was very small and she remembers not his name.

Julia had three sisters, Charlotte, Rose and Emoline Mack. The last names of the first two, Charlotte and Rose she could not recall.

As her memory is becoming faded, her thoughts wander from one thing to another and her speech is not very plain, the following is what I heard and understood during the interview.

"All de slaves work with neighbors; or like neighbors now-adays. I no work in de fiel, I slave in de house, maid to de mistress."

"After Yankees come, one sister came to Ohio with me."

"The slaves get a whippin if they run away."

"After Yankees come, my ole mother come home and all chillun together. I live with gramma and go home after work each day. Hired out doin maid work. All dis after Yankees come dat I live with gramma."

"Someone yell, 'Yankees are comin',' and de mistress tell me, she say 'You mus learn to be good and hones'.' I tole her, 'I am now'."

"No I nevah get no money foh work."

"I allways had good meals and was well taken care of. De Mrs. she nevah let me be sold."

"Sho we had a cook in de kichen and she was a slave too."

"Plantashun slaves had gahdens but not de house slaves. I allus had da bes clothes and bes meals, anyting I want to eat. De Mrs. like me and she like me and she say effen you want sompin ask foh it, anytime you want sompin or haff to have, get it. I didn suffer for enythin befoh dim Yankees come."

"After de Yankees come even de house people, de white people didn get shoes. But I hab some, I save. I have some othah shoes I didn dare go in de house with. Da had wood soles. Oh Lawde how da hurt mah feet. One day I come down stair too fas and slip an fall. Right den I tile de Mrs. I couldn wear dem big heavy shoes and besides da makes mah feet so sore."

"Bof de Mrs. and de Master sickly. An their chillun died. Da live in a big manshun house. Sho we had an overseer on de plantashun. De poor white people da live purty good, all dat I seed. It was a big plantashun. I can't remember how big but I know dat it was sho big. Da had lots an lots of slaves but I doan no zackly how many. Da scattered around de plantashun in diffren settlements. De horn blew every mohnin to wake up de fiel hans. Da gone to fiel long time foh I get up. De fiel hans work from dawn till dark, but evabody had good eats on holidays. No work jus eat and have good time."

"Da whipp dem slaves what run away."

"One day after de war was over and I come to Ohio, a man stop at mah house. I seem him and I know him too but I preten like I didn, so I say, 'I doan want ter buy nothin today' and he says 'Doan you know me?' Den I laugh an say sho I remember the day you wuz goin to whip me, you run affer me and I run to de Mrs. and she wouldn let you whip me. Now you bettah be careful or I get you."

"Sho I saw slaves sole. Da come from all ovah to buy an sell de slaves, chillun to ole men and women."

"De slaves walk and travel with carts and mules."

"De slaves on aukshun block dey went to highes bidder. One colored woman, all de men want her. She sold to de master who was de highes bidder, and den I saw her comin down de road singin 'I done got a home at las!'. She was half crazy. De maste he sole her and den Mrs. buy her back. They lef her work around de house. I used to make her work and make her shine things. She say I make her shine too much, but she haff crazy, an run away."

"No dey didn help colored folks read and write. Effn

dey saw you wif a book dey knock it down on de floor. Dey wouldn let dem learn."

"De aukshun allus held at Richmond. Plantashun owners come from all states to buy slaves and sell them."

"We had church an had to be dere every single Sunday. We read de Bible. De preacher did the readin. I can't read or write. We sho had good prayer meetins. Show nuf it was a Baptis church. I like any spiritual, all of dem."

"Dey batize all de young men and women, colored folks. Dey sing mos any spirtual, none in paticlar. A bell toll foh a funeral. At de baptizen do de pracher leads dem into de rivah, way in, den each one he stick dem clear under. I waz gonna be batize and couldn. Eva time sompin happin an I couldn. My ole mothah tole me I gotta be but I never did be baptize when Ise young in de south. De othah people befoh me all batized."

"A lot of de slaves come north. Dey run away cause dey didn want to be slaves, like I didn like what you do and I get mad, den you get mad an I run away."

"De pattyroller was a man who watched foh de slaves what try to run away. I see dem sneakin in an out dem bushes. When dey fine im de give im a good whippin."

"I nevah seed mush trouble between de whites and blacks when I live dare. Effen dey didn want you to get married, they wouldn let you. Dey had to ask de mastah and if he say no he mean it."

"When de Yankees were a comin through dem fiels, dey sho was awful. Dey take everythin and destroy what ever they could not take. De othah house slave bury the valables in de groun so de soldiers couldn fine em."

"One of the house slaves was allus havin her man comin to see her, so one day affer he lef, when I was makin fun and laughin at her de mistress she say, 'Why you picken on her?' I say, dat man comin here all the time hangin round, why doan he marry her."

"I was nevah lowed to go out an soshiate with de othah slaves much. I was in de house all time."

"I went to prayer meetins every Sunday monin and evenin."

"Sometimes dey could have a good time in de evenin and sometimes day couldn."

"Chrismas was a big time for everyone. In the manshun we allus had roast pig and a big feed. I could have anythin I want. New Years was the big aukshun day. All day hollerin on de block. Dey come from all ovah to Richmond to buy and sell de slaves."

"Butchern day sho was a big time. A big long table with de pigs laid out ready to be cut up."

"Lots of big parties an dances in de manshun. I nevah have time foh play. Mrs, she keep me busy and I work when I jus little girl and all mah life."

"Effen any slaves were sick dey come to de house for splies and medsin. De Mrs. and Master had de doctor if things were very bad."

"I'll nevah forget de soldiers comin. An old woman tole me de war done broke up, and I was settin on de porch. De Mrs. she say, 'Julia you ant stayin eneymore'. She tole me if I keep my money and save it she would give me some. An she done gave me a gold breast pin too. She was rich and had lots of money. After the war I wen home to my mother. She was half sick and she work too hard. On de way I met one slave woman who didn know she was even free."

"The Yankees were bad!"

"I didn get married right away. I worked out foh diffren famlies."

"After de war dare was good schools in de south. De free slaves had land effen dey knowed what to do with. I got married in the south to Richar Williams but I didn have no big weddin. I had an old preacher what knowed all bout de Bible, who married me. He was a good preacher. I was de mothah of eight chillun."

"Lincoln? Well I tell you I doan know. I didn have no thought about him but I seed him. I work in de house all de time and didn hear much about people outside."

"I doan believe in ghosts or hants. As foh dancin I enjoy it when I was young."

"I cant read and I thought to myself I thought there was a change comin. I sense that. I think de Lawd he does everythin right. De Lawd open my way. I think all people should be religious and know about de Lawd and his ways."

Her husband came to Wadsworth with the first group that came from Doylestown. The men came first then they sent for their families. Her husband came first them sent for her and the children. They settled in Wadsworth and built small shacks then later as times got better they bought properties.

This year is the 57th Anniversary of the Wadsworth Colored Baptist Church of which Julia Williams was a charter member. She is very close to 100 years old if not that now and lives at 160 Kyle Street, Wadsworth, Ohio.

United States. Work Projects Administration

Lees
Ohio Guide, Special
Ex-Slave Stories
August 17, 1937

JULIA WILLIAMS
(Supplementary Story)

JULIA WILLIAMS

"After de War deh had to pick their own livin' an seek homes.

"Shuah, deh expected de 40 acres of lan' an mules, but deh had to work foh dem."

"Shuah, deh got paht of de lan but de shuah had to work foh it.

"After de war deh had no place to stay an den deh went to so many diffrunt places. Some of dem today don't have settled places to live.

"Those owners who were good gave their slaves lan but de othahs jus turned de slaves loose to wander roun'. Othahs try to fine out where dere people were and went to them.

"One day I seed a man who was a doctor down dere, an' I says, 'You doktah now?' An says 'No, I doan doktah no mow.' I work foh him once when I was slave, few days durin de war. I say, 'Member that day you gonna lick me but you didn', you know I big woman an fight back. Now de war ovah and you can't do dat now'.

"Slaves didn get money unless deh work for it. Maybe a slave he would work long time before he get eny pay."

"Lak you hire me an you say you goin to pay me an then you don't. Lots of them hired slaves aftah de war and worked dem a long time sayin deh gwine pay and then when he ask for money, deh drive him away instead of payin him.

"Yes, some of de slaves were force to stay on de plantation. I see how some had to live." "They had homes for awhile but when deh wasen't able to pay dere rent cause deh weren't paid, deh were thrown out of dere houses." Some of dem didn't know when deh were free till long time after de Wah.

"When I were free, one mornin I seed the mistress and she ask me would I stay with her a couple years. I say, 'No I gonna find mah people an go dere.'

"Anyway, she had a young mister, a son, an he was mean to de slaves. I nebber lak him.

"Once I was sent to mah missys' brother for a time but I wouldn' stay dere: he too rough.

"No, deh didn't want you to learn out of books. My missy say one day when I was free, 'Now you can get your lessons.'

"I allus lowed to do what I wanted, take what I wanted, and eat what I wanted. Deh had lots of money but what good did it do them? Deh allus was sick.

"De poor soldiers had lots to go thru, even after de wah. Deh starvin and beggin and sick.

"De slaves had more meetins and gatherins aftah de war.

"On de plantation where I work dey had a great big horn blow every mornin to get de slaves up to de field, I allus get up soon after it blew, most allways, but this mornin dey blew de horn a long time an I says, 'what foh dey blow dat horn so long?' an den de mastah say, 'You all is free'. Den he says, ter me, 'What you all goin to do now', and I says, 'I'm goin to fine my mother.'

"One day a soldier stop me an says, 'Sister, where do you live?' I tole him, den he says, 'I'm hungry.' So I went an got him sompin to eat.

"One time I was to be sold de next day, but de missy tole the man who cried the block not to sell me, but deh sold my mother and I didn't see her after dat till just befoh de war ovah.

"All dat de slaves got after de war was loaned dem and dey had to work mighty hard to pay for dem. I saw a lot of poor people cut off from votin and dey off right now, I guess. I doan like it dat de woman vote. A woman ain't got no right votin, nowhow.

"Most of de slaves get pensions and are taken care of by their chillun."

"Ah doan know about de generation today, just suit yourself bout dat."

Julia Williams resides at 150 Kyle St., Wadsworth, Ohio.

United States. Work Projects Administration

Miriam Logan
Lebanon, Ohio
July 8th

Warren County, District 2

Story of REVEREND WILLIAMS, Aged 76,
Colored Methodist Minister,
Born Greenbriar County, West Virginia (Born 1859)

REVEREND WILLIAMS

"I was born on the estate of Miss Frances Cree, my mother's mistress. She had set my grandmother Delilah free with her sixteen children, so my mother was free when I was born, but my father was not.

"My father was butler to General Davis, nephew of Jefferson Davis. General Davis was wounded in the Civil War and came home to die. My father, Allen Williams was not free until the Emancipation."

"Grandmother Delilah belonged to Dr. Cree. Upon his death and the division of his estate, his maiden daughter came into possession of my grandmother, you understand. Miss Frances nor her brother Mr. Cam. ever married. Miss Frances was very religious, a Methodist, and she believed Grandmother Delilah should be free, and that we colored children should have schooling."

"Yes ma'm, we colored people had a church down there in West Virginia, and grandmother Delilah had a family Bible of her own. She had fourteen boys and two girls. My mother had sixteen children, two boys, fourteen girls. Of them—mother's children, you understand,—there were seven teachers and two ministers; all were educated—thanks to Miss Frances and to Miss Sands of Gallipolice. Mother lived to be ninety-seven years old. No, she was not a cook."

"In the south, you understand—there is the COLORED M.E. CHURCH, and the AFRICAN M.E. CHURCH, and the SOUTHERN METHODIST, and METHODIST EPISCOPAL CHURCHES of the white people. They say there will be UNION METHODIST of both white and colored people, but I don't believe there will be, for there is a great difference in beliefs, even today. SOUTHERN METHODIST do believe, do believe in slavery; while the Methodist to which Miss Frances Cree belonged did not believe in slavery. The Davis family, (one of the finest) did believe in slavery and they were good southern Methodist. Mr. Cam., Miss Frances brother was not so opposed to slavery as was Miss Frances. Miss Frances willed us to the care of her good Methodist friend Miss Eliza Sands of Ohio."

"Culture loosens predijuce. I do not believe in social equality at all myself; it cannot be; but we all must learn to keep to our own road, and bear Christian good will towards each other."

"I do not know of any colored people who are any more superstitious than are white people. They have the advantages of education now equally and are about on the same level. Of course illiterate whites and the illiterate colored man are apt to believe in charms. I do not remember of hearing of any particular superstitious among my church people that I could tell you about, no ma'm, I do not."

"In church music I hold that the good old hymns of John and of Charles Wesley are the best to be had. I don' like shouting 'Spirituals' show-off and carrying on—never did encourage it! Inward Grace will come out in your singing more than anything else you do, and the impression we carry away from your song and, from the singer are what I count." Read well, sing correctly, but first, last, remember real inward Grace is what shows forth the most in a song."

"In New Oreleans where I went to school,—(graduated in 1887 from the Freedman's Aid College)—there were 14 or 15 colored churches (methodist) in my youth. New Oreleans is one third colored in population, you understand. Some places in the south the colored outnumber the whites 30 to 1.

"I pastored St. Paul's church in Louieville, a church of close to 3,000 members. No'ma'm can't say just how old a church it is."

"To live a consecrated life, you'd better leave off dancing, drinking smoking and the movies. I've never been to a movie in my life. When I hear some of the programs colored folks put on the radio sometimes I feel just like going out to the woodshed and getting my axe and chopping up the radio, I do! It's natural and graceful to dance, but it is not natural or good to mill around in a low-minded smoky dance hall."

"I don't hold it right to put anybody out of church, no ma'm. No matter what they do, I don't believe in putting anybody out of church."

"My mother and her children were sent to Miss Eliza

Sands at Gallipolis, Ohio after Miss Frances Cree's death, at Miss Frances' request. Father did not go, no ma'm. He came later and finished his days with us."

"We went first to Point Pleasant, then up the river to Gallipolis."

"After we got there we went to school. A man got me a place in Cincinnati when I was twelve years old. I blacked boots and ran errands of the hotel office until I was thirteen; then I went to the FREEDMAN'S AID COLLEGE in N' Orleans; remained until I graduated. Shoemaking and carpentering were given to me for trades, but as young fellow I shipped on a freighter plying between New Orleans and Liverpool, thinking I would like to be a seaman. I was a mean tempered boy. As cook's helper one day, I got mad at the boatswain,—threw a pan of hot grease on him."

The crew wanted me put into irons, but the captain said 'no,—leave him in Liverpool soon as we land—in about a day or two. When I landed there they left me to be deported back to the States according to law."

"Yes, I had an aunt live to be 112 years old. She died at Granville (Ohio) some thirty years ago. We know her age from a paper on Dr. Cree's estate where she was listed as a child of twelve, and that had been one hundred years before."

"About the music now,—you see I'm used to thinking of religion as the working out of life in good deeds, not just a singing-show-off kind."

Some of the Spirituals are fine, but still I think Wesley hymns are best. I tell my folks that the good Lord isn't a deaf old gentleman that has to be shouted up to, or amused. I do think we colored people are a little too apt to want to show off in our singing sometimes."

"I was very small when we went away from Greenbriar County to Point Pleasant, and from there to Gallipolis by wagon. I do remember Mr. Cam. Cree. I was taring around the front lawn where he didn't want me; he was cross. I remember somebody taking me around the house, and thats all,-all that I can remember of the old Virginia home where my folks had belonged for several generations."

"I've pastored large churches in Louisville and St. Louis. In Ohio I have been at Glendale, and at Oxford,— other places. This old place was for sale on the court house steps one day when I happened to be in Lebanon. Five acres, yes ma'm. There's the corner stone with 1822—age of the house. My sight is poor, can't read, so I do not try to preach much anymore, but I help in church in any way that I am needed, keep busy and happy always! I am able to garden and enjoy life every day. Certainly my life has been a fortunate one in my mother's belonging to Miss Frances Cree. I have been a minister some forty years. I graduated from Wilberforce College."

This colored minister has a five acre plot of ground and an old brick house located at the corporation line of the village of Lebanon. He is a medium sized man. Talks very fast. A writer could turn in about 40 pages on an interview with him, but he is very much in earnest about his beliefs. He seems to be rather nervous and has very poor sight. His wife is yellow in color, and has a decidedly oriental cast of face. She is as silent, as he is talkative, and from general appearances of her home she is a very neat housekeeper. Neither of them speak in dialect at all. Wade Glenn does not speak in dialect, although he is from North Carolina.

Ex-Slaves
Stark County, District 5
Aug 13, 1937

WILLIAM WILLIAMS, Ex-Slave

WILLIAM WILLIAMS

"I was born a slave in Caswell County, North Carolina, April 14, 1857. My mother's name was Sarah Hunt and her master's name was Taz Hunt. I did not know who my father was until after the war. When I was about 11 years old I went to work on a farm for Thomas Williams and he told me he was my father. When I was born he was a slave on the plantation next to Hunt's place and was owned by John Jefferson. Jefferson sold my father after I was born but I do not know his last master's name.

My father and mother were never married. They just had the permission of the two slave owners to live together and I became the property of my father's master, John Jefferson until I was sold. After the war my mother joined my father on his little farm and it was then I first learned he was my father.

I was sold when I was 3 years old but I don't remember the name of the man that bought me.

After the war my father got 100 acres and a team of mules to farm on shares, the master furnishing the food for the first year and at the end of the second year he had the privilege of buying the land at $1.00 per acre.

When I was a boy I played with other slave children

and sometimes with the master's children and what little education I have I got from them. No, I can't read or write but I can figure 'like the devil'.

The plantation of John Jefferson was one of the biggest in the south, it had 2200 acres and he owned about 2000 slaves.

I was too young to remember anything about the slave days although I do remember that I never saw a pair of shoes until I was old enough to work. My father was a cobbler and I used to have to whittle out shoe pegs for him and I had to walk sometimes six miles to get pine knots which we lit at night so my mother could see to work.

I did not stay with my father and mother long as I was only about 14 when I started north. I worked for farmers every place I could find work and sometimes would work a month or maybe two. The last farmer I worked for I stayed a year and I got my board and room and five dollars a month which was paid at the end of every six months. I stayed in Pennsylvania for some years and came to Canton in 1884. I have always worked at farm work except now and then in a factory.

I had two brothers, Dan and Tom, and one sister, Dora, but I never heard from them or saw them after the war. I have been married twice. My first wife was Sally Dillis Blaire and we were married in 1889. I got a divorce a few years later and I don't know whatever became of her. My second wife is still living. Her name was Kattie Belle Reed and I married her in 1907. No, I never had any children.

I don't believe I had a bed when I was a slave as I don't remember any. At home, after the war, my mother and father's bed was made of wood with ropes stretched across with a straw tick on top. 'Us kids' slept under this bed on a 'trundle' bed so that at night my mother could just reach down and look after any one of us if we were sick or anything.

I was raised on ash cakes, yams and butter milk. These ash cakes were small balls made of dough and my mother would rake the ashes out of the fire place and lay these balls on the hot coals and then cover them over with the ashes again. When they were done we would take 'em out, clean off the ashes and eat them. We used to cook chicken by first cleaning it, but leaving the feathers on, then cover it with clay and lay it in a hole filled with hot coals. When it was done we would just knock off the clay and the feathers would come off with it.

When I was a 'kid' I wore nothing but a 'three cornered rag' and my mother made all my clothes as I grew older. No, the slaves never knew what underwear was.

We didn't have any clocks to go by; we just went to work when it was light enough and quit when it was too dark to see. When any slaves took sick they called in a nigger mammy who used roots and herbs, that is, unless they were bad sick, then the overseer would call a regular doctor.

When some slave died no one quit work except relatives and they stopped just long enough to go to the funeral. The coffins were made on the plantation, these were just rough pine board boxes, and the bodies were buried in the grave yard on the plantation.

The overseer on the Jefferson plantation, so my father told me, would not allow the slaves to pray and I never saw a bible until after I came north. This overseer was not a religious man and would whip a slave if he found him praying.

The slaves were allowed to sing and dance but were not allowed to play games, but we did play marbles and cards on the quiet. If we wandered too far from the plantation we were chased and when they caught us they put us in the stockade. Some of the slaves escaped and as soon as the overseer found this out they would turn the blood hounds loose. If they caught any runaway slaves they would whip them and then sell them, they would never keep a slave who tried to run away."

NOTE: Mr. Williams and his wife are supported by the Old Age Pension. Interviewed by Chas. McCullough.

Slave Narratives

www.ingramcontent.com/pod-product-compliance
Lightning Source LLC
Chambersburg PA
CBHW070755100426
42742CB00012B/2147